THE DOMESTIC DIVA'S
Party
COOKBOOK

Patricia F. Hemming
and
Keely J. Hemming

CFI
Springville, Utah

ISBN: 1-55517-887-1
v.1

Published by CFI,
an imprint of Cedar Fort, Inc.
925 N. Main Springville, Utah, 84663
www.cedarfort.com

Distributed by:

Cover and book design by Nicole Williams
Cover design © 2005 by Lyle Mortimer

Printed in China
10 9 8 7 6 5 4 3 2 1

Printed on acid-free paper

Our book is lovingly dedicated to Thomas
and Beverly Felt. Patricia's parents and
Keely's grandparents. You
have taught us from your
examples how important
family and friends
are as we have celebrated life
with parties and get-togethers. So
many of our treasured memories have
been created during those moments. We look
forward to sharing many more celebrations
with you. We love you!

Contents

Preface

What is the essence of nostalgia? Can an aroma, a word, or a song transport you to a scene from your past? Have you ever tasted a memory?

Memories are treasures we gather along life's way and tuck into our hearts. They help define who we are. They add richness and fullness to our lives, making each day extraordinary in its own way.

Because many of our remembrances are created at home, some of the most meaningful gifts we can give our families are valuable memories that they will carry forever in their hearts. We create memories by celebrating special occasions with our families, but even more important, by celebrating the ordinary days.

As we began writing this book, we reminisced. The parties, the laughter, the favorite foods, and the happy times welled up in our hearts and flowed onto these pages. What a pleasure it has been.

The *Domestic Diva's Party Cookbook* is more than a cookbook or an idea book. It's a collection of possibilities, opportunities, and, we hope, a source of inspiration for celebrations. Our aim is to encourage you and present you with ideas. You will no doubt take it from there and add your own personal touches.

Most of the get-together ideas in this book can be held any time of the year, not just during the month they appear. You can choose from numerous entertaining suggestions and many recipes. You may incorporate them all or just a few, adding your own style and flair. As you try an idea or two, remember:

- Focus on the meaningful.
- Perfection is verboten.
- Enjoy the celebration.

Acknowledgments

Our heartfelt thanks to family and friends who have celebrated with us and shared themselves, including their recipes, ideas, and encouragement: Mom (Gram), Non, LeeAnn, Rebecca, Margaret, Marge, Jennifer, Rachel, Missy, Jean, Carole, Dawn, Carma, Lorraine, Kristine, Marsha, Meg, Allison, Nelda, and Connie.

Thanks also to Michael, husband and father, who has spent months tasting recipes and providing specialized computer services and all around moral support.

Secrets for Having Fun at Your Own Party

Entertaining and sharing meals can be as natural and sincere as anything else you do. The primary importance is the bringing together of the people you care about to share food, laughter and the company of each other.

Plan ahead—make a list and include the following:

• Type of party

• Guest List—Keep the number manageable, no more than twelve to sixteen people for a sit-down dinner party, and around twenty to twenty-five for a buffet.

• Menu—Plan only what you can accomplish easily and what you are comfortable with. If time is at a premium, make one great dish and use deli or bakery items to supplement. Use your special recipes time and time again. Guests will look forward to the traditional favorites. Include foods with contrasting colors, textures and temperatures. Never try out a new recipe on your guests; it's too stressful for you. Use many recipes that can be prepared ahead of time. Simplify.

• Supplies Needed—Groceries, serving dishes, cutlery, dishes, napkins, candles, centerpieces, music, camera and film. Don't overspend. Use what you have. Entertaining doesn't need to be expensive. Make your guests feel special and have fun. That's what your guests will long remember.

• Things to do—Shop, order any specialty dishes from the store that you are going to serve, straighten the house, and clean a bathroom (you'll probably need to clean the house after the party, so don't go to great lengths to clean before the party). Don't wait until the house is clean to have a party—you'll always be waiting. Remember your guests are the people you love; they are coming to see you, not the house.

• Be prepared with a "Plan B"—you never know when something unexpected will happen. If need be take the party outside, order a pizza, and have a dinner on the hood of your car, or in case of rain, bring the party inside.

The most important person at your party is you!

• Wear your favorite and most comfortable clothes (no, sweats don't count).

• Be at the door to greet each guest warmly.

• Introduce each guest to the others if they are not acquainted, and start up a conversation.

• If there's a disaster in the kitchen, remember: you do not need to be a great cook to be a great hostess. Whatever happens, try to fix it without anyone noticing. If it is obvious, remember to laugh—these are your friends and family.

• Be gracious, warm, and happy.

• Most importantly: Relax and have fun!

CELEBRATE LAUGHTER

January

Great is the human who has not lost his childlike heart. —Mencius

Silly Social

Pull out all the stops and be as silly as you can be. It's not often an opportunity like this presents itself, so enjoy it to the fullest.

IDEAS

• Mail or hand deliver invitations to each guest or couple, inviting them to your Silly Social. Encourage them to wear the funniest combination of clothing they own, telling them a prize will be awarded to the silliest. Invite them to dinner, but tell them they will need to bring the ingredients for dinner and also help prepare it. Assign each couple or person to bring one of the ingredients for the "Group Effort Soup" (you provide the hamburger).

• Let your imagination run wild as you set the table. Mix and match paper cups, paper plates and napkins (or paper towels) from a variety of holidays. A decorated paper tablecloth would complete the look. Some wilted flowers in a vase would be a nice addition (florists are usually glad to give you their wilted flowers).

• When the guests arrive direct them to the kitchen and assign them a task to help with dinner. Some could brown the hamburger, others peel and cut the vegetables and others could get the bread sticks ready. Have some prepared fresh vegetables in a container and some cheese and crackers for your guests to munch on as they are cooking.

• Take candid pictures of your company.

• After dinner, clean up will be a breeze and leave plenty of time to watch a silly movie.

• Award the silliest get-up with a prize.

Menu

Rabbit Food (fresh vegetable plate)
Cheese and Crackers
Group-Effort Soup
Crunchy Cheese Sticks (bread sticks)
Dirt Cups
or Chocolate Cookie Stack

Group-Effort Soup

INGREDIENTS
1 pound ground beef
1 cup chopped onion
4 cups hot water
1½ cups chopped celery
1½ cups chopped carrots
1½ cups quartered potatoes
2 teaspoons salt
½ teaspoon pepper
1 bay leaf, crumbled
1 can whole tomatoes
1 tablespoon beef bouillon

Brown beef; add onion and cook until softened. Add the rest of the ingredients, except the tomatoes. Bring to a boil, cover and simmer 20 minutes. Add tomatoes, and if necessary, more water; simmer 10 minutes longer.

Yield: 4–6 servings.

Crunchy Cheese Sticks

INGREDIENTS
24 frozen dinner rolls, thawed but still cold (thaw in refrigerator)
½ cup butter
½ teaspoon garlic salt
1 cup shredded mild cheddar cheese
1 cup shredded mozzarella cheese
½ cup Parmesan cheese
2 teaspoons parsley flakes

Preheat oven to 350 degrees. Combine butter and garlic salt in a bowl. In another bowl combine the cheeses and parsley flakes. Shape each roll into a rope 5 inches long. Dip in butter mixture and then roll in cheese mixture. Place on a cookie sheet and let rise 30 minutes. Bake 15 to 20 minutes until cheese starts to brown. Serve warm.
Yield: 24 sticks.

Dirt Cups

INGREDIENTS
1 package instant chocolate pudding, prepared as directed on package
½ package chocolate sandwich cookies, crushed
Candy gummy worms (optional)

Partially fill 6 to 8 clear plastic glasses with chocolate pudding. Sprinkle crushed cookies over the top. Candy worms crawling out of the glasses are a nice finishing touch.
Yield: 6–8 servings.

Chocolate Cookie Stack

1 pint whipping cream
$2/3$ cup powdered sugar
1 teaspoon vanilla
Chocolate wafer cookies
2 large bananas

Whip cream; add sugar and vanilla. Line a square baking pan with chocolate wafers; slice bananas over cookies. Frost banana layer with whipped cream. Repeat process for a second layer. Sprinkle top with crushed cookies. Cover and store in refrigerator.
Yield: 8–9 servings.

Baggy Pants Party

It has often been said that laughter is a remedy for the body and soul, medical science has confirmed it. Laughter is just plain good for us. The ability to laugh with others and not take ourselves too seriously is one of life's pleasures. Share an evening of laughter with family and friends for an out-of-the-ordinary pizza dinner and a party they will never forget.

IDEAS

• When inviting your guests to the party, ask them to be sure to wear baggy pants so they will be able to eats lots and lots of pizza. The baggier the pants, the better. (Gramps "wore" a large, orange leaf bag on each leg and tied them at his waist with rope.) Mention that prizes will be awarded.

• A picture is worth a thousand words, and there will be many "you've got to see it to believe it" photo opportunities. So, have plenty of film. Take pictures of each of your guests so they will have a lasting reminder of the evening.

• After all the guests arrive, award prizes for the baggiest pants, the most outlandish, the funniest, the most creative, the most stylish, and so forth. Have enough prizes to give everyone an award. The dollar stores are great places to look for inexpensive and fun prizes. Some awards could be suspenders, a belt, a rope (to hold their pants up) a pizza pan, or a pizza cutter. You'll think of some winners.

• After dinner, continue the laughter by playing "The Bean Game." Give everyone a plastic bag with three times as many beans as players. The more beans, the longer the game lasts. (The beans can be counted out days before the party.) Have everyone sit on chairs forming a circle.

In the middle of the circle place a large container like a wide mouth jar or metal tub. As the host or hostess, start the game by saying something you've never done before. For instance, "I've never had a speeding ticket." Then, everyone who has ever received a speeding ticket throws one of their beans into the container in the middle of the circle.

Go around the circle in this fashion, as many times as desired. The person with the most beans left is the winner.

Menu

Marinated Vegetables

Stuffed Crust Pizza

Frypan Pizza

Chicken BLT Pizza

Green Salad with Dijon Vinaigrette Dressing

Ice Cream Pie

Italian Sodas

Marinated Vegetables

3 large ribs celery, cut into strips

3 medium carrots, peeled and cut into strips

24 cherry tomatoes

1 jar (14¾ ounces) marinated artichoke hearts, drained

1 can (6 ounces) large pitted olives, drained

1 can (7 ounces) green olives, drained

2 cups broccoli florets

2 medium cucumbers, peeled and sliced in rounds

2 cups cauliflowerettes

1½ cups salad oil

2/3 cup white vinegar

1 teaspoon salt

1 teaspoon garlic powder

1/8 teaspoon pepper

2 teaspoon sugar

In a large bowl combine oil, vinegar, salt, garlic powder, pepper and sugar. Mix well and add vegetables. Marinate in covered bowl overnight before serving.

Yield: 8 servings.

Stuffed Crust Pizza

INGREDIENTS
1 pound frozen white bread dough (thawed)
Flour
¼ teaspoon yellow cornmeal
3 ounces pepperoni, sliced
7 sticks of string cheese
1 teaspoon olive oil
½ cup prepared pizza, marinara, or spaghetti sauce
1½ cups mozzarella cheese, shredded
2 ounces pepperoni, sliced
¼ cup fresh Parmesan cheese, grated
1 teaspoon dried oregano leaves

Preheat oven to 450 degrees. On a floured surface, roll out the thawed dough into a 14 to 15 inch circle. Lightly spray a 12-inch pizza pan. Sprinkle the cornmeal over the pan and place the crust on the pan, the edges will hang over the sides. Arrange the pepperoni and string cheese around the outer edge. Fold the edge of the crust over to enclose the pepperoni and cheese. Press into bottom of crust and brush with the olive oil. Prick the center crust with fork tines. Bake for 7 to 10 minutes. Remove from the oven and fill by spreading the sauce over center of crust, arrange the cheese over sauce, then pepperoni slices over all. Top with Parmesan cheese and oregano leaves. Return to oven for 7 more minutes or until golden brown and bubbly over the top. Remove from oven. Cut into wedges and serve immediately.
Yield: 4 to 6 servings.

Frypan Pizza

INGREDIENTS

1 package Hot Roll Mix
1 can (8 ounces) pizza sauce
½ pound mozzarella cheese, shredded
1 can (4 ounces) mushrooms, drained and sliced
½ pound Italian sausage or ground beef, cooked
Grated Parmesan cheese
Chopped parsley
Oregano

Prepare dough as directed on package. Place in greased bowl; let rise until double in bulk, about 40 minutes. Divide in half, set aside half for another pizza. Butter hands generously and pat out dough to cover cold bottom of well-greased electric frypan, about ¼ inch up on sides. Add sauce, spreading over surface. Top with cheese, sliced mushrooms, and cooked meat. Sprinkle with Parmesan cheese, parsley and a bit of oregano. Cover frypan, close vent, set dial at 280 degrees. Bake for 15 to 17 minutes or until dough is set. Slide out with spatula. Cut with pizza cutter into squares. Serve piping hot.

Chicken BLT Pizza

INGREDIENTS

1 large (14 ounces) prepared Italian pizza crust
Butter to spread on crust
2 cups shredded mozzarella cheese
2 chicken breasts, cooked and cubed
6 slices bacon, cooked and cut into small pieces
Shredded lettuce
Mayonnaise
Diced tomato
Cubed avocado

Preheat oven to 450 degrees. Place crust on a cookie sheet. Lightly spread crust with butter. Sprinkle crust with cheese, then chicken and bacon. Bake for 6 to 7 minutes or until cheese is melted. While pizza is baking, combine the lettuce with enough mayonnaise to moisten it well. Remove pizza from oven and top with lettuce mixture, diced tomato, and cubed avocado. Cut and serve immediately.

Yield: 4 to 6 servings.

DiJon Vinaigrette Dressing

I N G R E D I E N T S
¼ cup red wine vinegar
½ teaspoon salt
2 tablespoons Dijon mustard, less for milder flavor
¼ teaspoon pepper
¾ cup salad oil

Combine all but the oil in a blender or processor; drizzle the oil in while the machine is going.

VARIATIONS

Use as a salad dressing or to marinate beef or chicken overnight. Add a little yogurt or sour cream and use as a dressing for a shredded carrot, apple, and onion salad. Try cubed roast beef and blanched cubed broccoli with a few crushed capers for a main meal salad. Could be used with yogurt as a tart fruit salad dressing.

Ice Cream Pie

I N G R E D I E N T S
1 prepared cookie crumb piecrust
1 to 1½ quarts ice cream (same flavor or two different kinds)
Ice cream topping
Crushed candies, fruit, nuts, sprinkles, or whipped cream (optional)

Thaw ice cream in the refrigerator until soft enough to spoon into piecrust. Freeze until firm; use plastic wrap to cover pie. Remove from freezer 5 minutes before serving. Use a warm knife to slice the pie.

Yield: 6 to 8 servings.

Tip: Pie will keep in freezer for several days so can be made well ahead of time.

THESE ARE OUR FAVORITE COMBINATIONS:

Layer in order given: Chocolate crust, ½ quart vanilla ice cream, chocolate ice cream topping, 1 quart chocolate ice cream (piled high), crushed English toffee candy bars sprinkled on top.

• Chocolate crust, ½ quart chocolate ice cream, chocolate ice cream topping, 1 quart peppermint ice cream (piled high), crushed peppermint candies sprinkled on top.

• Butter cookie crust, ½ quart chocolate or vanilla ice cream, cubed bananas, chocolate or caramel topping, 1 quart strawberry ice cream (piled high). Just before serving top with additional ice cream topping and whipped cream.

• Butter cookie crust, ½ quart vanilla ice cream, caramel topping, 1 quart caramel pecan, English toffee, or pralines and cream ice cream, chopped nuts sprinkled on top.

Italian Soda

INGREDIENTS

1 ounces flavored Italian syrup
(raspberry, peach, strawberry and boysenberry are our favorites)
½ ounce half and half
Seltzer or club soda
Ice

To a tall glass add ice, syrup of your choice and half and half. Fill the glass to the top with seltzer or soda. Stir and serve.

Yield: 1 serving.

Tip: The Italian syrups are available in many grocery stores, usually in the hot beverage aisle, and in most kitchen shops.

CELEBRATE LOVE

February

A friend knows the song in my heart and sings it to me when my memory fails.—Donna Roberts

A Very Best Friend's Day

One of the most beautiful things about friendship is that it can transcend traditional roles. A friend can be anyone—mother, sister, daughter, husband, or other family member. If we want our friendships to last and grow, we need to give of ourselves in caring for and maintaining them. As we spend time together, help each other, and enjoy each other's company, we strengthen those bonds. Having a friend is one of the greatest gifts you've ever had. Cherish it. Plan an entire day to spend with your best friend. Allow yourselves time to laugh, exchange stories, and share dreams without the pressure of a time limit.

IDEAS

• Start the day out with an early breakfast or a brunch that you fix together. It has been said, "Friendships, like geraniums, grow best in the kitchen."

• Plan what you are going to do on your day together well ahead of time so after breakfast you can start right away. The plans don't need to be extravagant, costly, or extensive, just do something together you both enjoy.

Here are a few ideas to consider:

• Do a craft project together. Make refrigerator magnets by clipping off the shank part of a plastic button (found at craft stores) and hot gluing a ½-inch round magnet onto the back of the button. Themed buttons work up well. Our favorites are the silver or gold colored heart shaped buttons. Just make sure the button covers the magnet.

• Make a bevy of personalized ribbons by writing names or messages on satin ribbon with a gel pen, or on acetate ribbon with an opaque, metallic ink marker.

• Showcase your creativity and compile two scrapbooks, one for each of you, celebrating your time spent together from the previous year. Be sure to take lots of pictures this year so you'll have more to add to your books next time.

• If you're not into scrapbooking, making your own greeting cards is a fun way to use all the exquisite papers and accessories available.

• Indulge yourselves with a pedicure.

• Drive to a neighboring town to get an ice cream cone.

• Go to a "chick flick."

• Visit a museum.

• Get a makeover.

• Play tennis.

• Spend some time shopping, looking for bargains or treasures.

• Explore a brand-new store.

• Go on a hike.

• Go to a day spa.

Menu

Croissant French Toast with Vanilla Sauce and Berries
Or Chocolate French Toast with Butter Syrup
Or Bacon Quiche Tarts with Berries and Crème Fraîche
Frozen Fruit Cocktail
Sugared Raisin Cookies (for a snack later in the day)

Croissant French Toast

INGREDIENTS
Several croissant halves per person
6 to 8 eggs, beaten

Prepare vanilla sauce first (recipe on next page). It can be made up to a day ahead and refrigerated. Warm before serving. To prepare the Croissant French Toast, slit the croissants in half and dip in beaten egg. Allow several croissant halves per person. Cook on an electric griddle or in a fry pan until both sides are set. Top with berries if desired and serve with vanilla sauce.

Vanilla Sauce

INGREDIENTS
1 tablespoon flour
4 egg yolks
1 tablespoon vanilla
2 cups whipping cream
½ cup sugar
2 scoops vanilla ice cream

In a small bowl combine flour, egg yolks, and vanilla; set aside. In a saucepan combine cream and sugar; bring to a boil over medium heat. Stir a small amount of cream mixture into the egg mixture. Return all to pan. Stirring constantly, bring to a gentle boil; cook and stir for two minutes. Remove from heat and stir in vanilla ice cream until melted. Serve warm.

Chocolate French Toast

1 cup whipping cream
1/3 cup semisweet chocolate chips
3 large eggs
1 teaspoon vanilla extract
1 loaf of white or egg bread, cut in 1/2-inch thick slices
2 tablespoons butter

Place cream and chocolate chips in a glass bowl. Microwave until chocolate is soft, 1 to 1½ minutes. Stir to combine; let cool. In a large bowl, beat together eggs, vanilla, and chocolate mixture. (Mixture may be prepared to this point, covered and refrigerated overnight. Stir well before using.) Soak bread in egg mixture for about 2 minutes on each side. Melt butter in a large skillet over medium heat or on an electric griddle. Cook until bread is toasted and firm on both sides. Serve warm.

Yield: 8 to 10 slices.

Butter Syrup

1 cup butter
½ cup buttermilk
1 cup sugar
1 teaspoon vanilla
1 teaspoon baking soda

Combine butter, buttermilk, and sugar in a saucepan and heat slowly to dissolve sugar. Add vanilla and baking soda, stirring to combine. Serve warm over French toast, pancakes, or waffles.

Bacon Quiche Tarts

I N G R E D I E N T S

6 ounces cream cheese, softened
5 teaspoons milk
2 eggs
½ cup shredded Colby cheese
2 tablespoons diced green peppers, optional
1 tablespoon diced onion, optional
1 tube (8 ounces) refrigerated crescent rolls
5 bacon strips, cooked and crumbled

Preheat oven to 375 degrees. In a small bowl, beat cream cheese and milk until smooth. Add eggs, cheese, green pepper, and onion; mix well. Separate dough into eight triangles; press onto the bottom and up the sides of eight greased muffin cups. Sprinkle half of the bacon into cups. Pour egg mixture over the bacon; top with remaining bacon. Bake for 20 minutes. Serve warm.

Yield: 8 servings.

Crème Fraiche

1 cup heavy cream (not ultra pasteurized)
1 cup dairy sour cream

Whisk heavy cream and sour cream together in a bowl. Cover loosely with plastic wrap and let stand in the kitchen (or other reasonably warm spot) overnight, or until thickened. In cold weather this may take as long as 24 hours. Cover and refrigerate for at least 4 hours, after which the crème fraiche will be quite thick. The tart flavor will continue to develop as the crème fraiche sits in the refrigerator.

Yield: 2 cups.

Tip: Great served with fresh berries.

Frozen Fruit Cocktail

2 cups sugar
3 pounds peaches (12 medium or 6 cups) peeled and sliced
1 pound seedless green grapes
1²/₃ cups crushed pineapple
Juice of 2 lemons (¹/₃ cup)
Juice of 3 oranges (1 cup)

Cover peaches with sugar. Allow to stand until juice begins to flow. Add remaining ingredients and mix gently until sugar is dissolved. Pack in freezer containers leaving ½-inch head space. Seal and freeze.

Yield: 5 to 6 pints.

Tip: Remove from freezer about 30 to 45 minutes before serving to partially thaw mixture. Do not let it fully thaw. Fruit is much tastier when still partially frozen.

Sugared Raisin Cookies

2 cups raisins

1 cup butter

1½ cups sugar

3 eggs

3½ cups flour

1 teaspoon soda

1 teaspoon salt

1 teaspoon vanilla

Boil raisins in 1 cup water until half of liquid is gone. Let it get cold. Cream butter and sugar until fluffy and add eggs, one at a time, beating well after each addition. Add vanilla. Combine flour, salt, and soda. Add 1 tablespoon of the mixture at a time to sugar mixture using an electric mixer. Fold in the raisins. Chill in refrigerator overnight. Make cookies from a tablespoon of dough. Form into a ball and then roll in sugar. Place on cookie sheet and flatten each ball with a spatula.

Bake at 375 degrees for 10 to 15 minutes.

A Little Romance–
Dinner For Two

Valentine's Day has long been the designated time for sweethearts to celebrate their love and enjoy some together time with a romantic dinner. But, there are many other moments to celebrate: anniversaries, promotions, birthdays, any kind of good news, or merely "because." Look beyond the obvious and create your own romantic days of the heart. The ideas presented below also work well for dinner before high school and college dances.

IDEAS

• While planning your dinner use your imagination and entertain the idea of serving the meal somewhere other than the kitchen or dinning room. With a card table, two folding chairs, and a few candles, the possibilities are endless. During the winter months, set the table in front of a roaring fire in the fireplace, or in the living room surrounded by a myriad of small white Christmas lights. When the weather is warm outside, take your card table to the deck, or the backyard lawn, the park, or even atop a hill overlooking the city.

• Ambience is an integral part of creating a romantic evening.

A white tablecloth, candles, music, and a flower or two are the basic elements. Formality heightens expectation. Candles can range from one taper or votive on the table to pillar candles and votives scattered all around the room. The music can be generated from a battery operated CD player, or if you have a friend that plays the guitar or violin, a serenade would be unforgettable.

• For a personal touch, create and play your own CD full of songs that are meaningful to you as a couple. A single red rose placed beside each napkin or a beautiful bouquet both convey the message, "I love you."

• If your dinner destination is away from

home, local restaurant supply businesses and many grocery stores sell disposable containers with lids for easy transport of food.

• After Valentine's Day, pick up sale items that have a heart theme such as: heart dishes, a heart pan, candles, little gift bags, napkins and the list goes on. All of these items can be stored and put to good use for future romantic dinners.

Menu

Stuffed Pork Chops

Oriental Peas

Candied Yams

Lettuce Wedges drizzled with favorite dressing

Refrigerator Rolls

Chocolate Dipped Strawberries

Virginia Fudge

Non-Alcoholic Sparkling Cider

Stuffed Pork Chops

INGREDIENTS

2 tablespoons butter

2 tablespoons finely chopped onion

4 teaspoons sage

4 teaspoons crushed basil leaves

1 tablespoon parsley flakes

1½ cups bread cubes

6 pork chops (1-inch thick. Ask the butcher to cut a pocket in each chop)

¼ cup onion soup mix

½ cup water

Melt butter, add onion, sage, basil, and parsley. Sauté mixture until onion is golden. Toss with bread cubes. Stuff mixture into pork chop pockets. Brown chops in a small amount of butter, then place in an oblong baking or casserole dish. Sprinkle with onion soup mix. Pour water over chops; cover and bake at 325 degrees for 1 hour or until tender.

Yield: 6 servings.

Tip: The pork chops could be stuffed earlier in the day, refrigerated, and then browned and baked. Stuffed, unbaked pork chops can be frozen for later use. Wrap each chop individually in freezer paper and then foil and put each in a freezer plastic bag. Will freeze well for 3 to 4 months.

Oriental Peas

I N G R E D I E N T S

1 package (10 ounces) frozen peas
4 tablespoons butter
1 can (8 ounces) sliced water chestnuts, drained

Cook peas according to package directions. Combine butter and water chestnuts in a saucepan. Cook until butter turns a caramel color. Pour mixture over peas. Garnish with carrot curls. Serve immediately.

Yield: 4 servings.

Candied Yams

INGREDIENTS
½ pound brown sugar
½ cup butter
6 yams, cooked, peeled and cut into fourths

Combine sugar and butter in an electric fry pan and stir until syrupy. Bring to a boil, reduce heat, add yams and simmer for about 1 hour. The longer the yams simmer, the more candied they are.

Refrigerator Rolls

INGREDIENTS

2 tablespoons dry yeast

½ cup lukewarm water

1 cup shortening

¾ cup sugar

2 teaspoons salt

1 cup boiling water

4 eggs, beaten

8 cups sifted flour

½ cup powdered milk

1 cup cold water

In a large bowl, soften yeast in warm water. Cream shortening, sugar, and salt; add boiling water and beat until smooth. Add the softened yeast, beaten eggs, and mix well. Add flour and powdered milk alternately with cold water, beating well after each addition. Cover tightly with plastic wrap. Place in refrigerator overnight. Roll out ¼ to 3/8-inches thick for rolls. Bake 10 to 12 minutes in a 400 degree oven.

Tip: Batch freeze extra rolls before baking. Place in a freezer bag and keep for later use.

Chocolate Dipped Strawberries

INGREDIENTS
1 bag (6 ounces) semisweet chocolate chips
1 tablespoon shortening
Strawberries, washed and dried thoroughly
Colored sugars, decors, crushed candies, vanilla-flavored coating (optional)

Line a jelly roll pan with waxed paper. Heat chocolate chips and shortening in a heavy saucepan over low heat, or in the microwave, stirring frequently until smooth. Remove from heat. Dip strawberries three-quarters of the way into chocolate, and place on waxed paper. Sprinkle with sugar, decors, or candies, or drizzle with melted vanilla-flavored coating, if desired. Refrigerate uncovered about 30 minutes or until chocolate is firm.

Yield: 2 to 3 dozen strawberries.

Tip: Other fruits such as red grapes, cherries, raspberries, or small cookies are also delicious dipped.

Virginia Fudge

INGREDIENTS

1 can (12 ounces) evaporated milk

½ cup butter

2 tablespoons light corn syrup

2 cups firmly packed brown sugar

1 cup granulated sugar

1 teaspoon vanilla (could use maple)

2 cups pecans

Set aside an ungreased 9x13 pan. In a heavy pan, combine milk, butter, corn syrup, and sugars. Cook over medium heat, stirring occasionally with a wooden spoon, until mixture comes to a boil. Wash down sides of pan with a wet pastry brush. Cook to 228 degrees. Pour, without scraping, into pan. Cool until lukewarm. Add vanilla; stir with a wooden spoon until mixture thickens. Add nuts and continue stirring until candy loses its gloss. Scrape onto plastic wrap. Pat into a loaf shape about 9x5 inches. Wrap in plastic and foil and store in refrigerator.

CELEBRATE TALENT

March

Every artist was first an amateur.—Ralph Waldo Emerson

You Are Special Night

Each year recognize the accomplishments, progress, successes, or achievements of each family member. Let them take center stage, live in the moment and feel truly special.

IDEAS

• Grandparents could be invited to share in this evening of celebration.

Remember to include married children and their spouses, and children away from home. If the distance is too far to travel, recognize each by a phone call during the party, or a letter afterwards.

• Invite someone to emcee the event.

• Make or purchase an inexpensive award for everyone. Candy bar notes are a lot of fun to make. Use the words on a candy bar to help convey a message. For instance: "Bobby, 'Bar None,' you are the best basketball player in the 'Milky Way,'" or, "Amy, you have been a 'Life Saver' to our family this year." Instead of candy bar notes, the dollar stores have a wide variety of items that could be used for awards.

• After dinner, ask each family member to stand while the emcee reads their name, the award to be given, and the reason for the award. Allow time for each recipient to respond or give a speech.

• As parents, express your feelings about each child and explain why they are special to you.

• Take lots of pictures! Tip: If you don't

scrapbook, there are many other ways to organize your pictures. They can be put onto a CD, filed in photo boxes, or slipped into acid free plastic jackets and put into a book. Whatever the method of preservation, in the years to come your photos will be priceless to you and will bring back a flood of memories.

Menu

Chicken and Rice

Lemon Vegetables

Waldorf Salad

Snowflake Biscuits

Sour Cream Banana Cake with Quick Caramel Frosting

Chicken and Rice

INGREDIENTS

1 tablespoons butter
3 to 4 skinless, boneless chicken breasts
1 can cream of chicken soup
$1^2/_3$ cup milk
$1^1/_3$ cup uncooked instant rice

Heat butter in a frying pan over medium heat. Add chicken and cook 10 minutes or until browned. Set chicken aside. Add soup and milk to frypan and bring to a boil. Stir in rice. Place chicken on the rice. Reduce heat to low. Cover and cook 5 minutes, or until chicken is done.

Lemon Vegetables

¼ cup butter

3 green onions, chopped

1 package (10 ounces) frozen cauliflower

2 packages (10 ounces each) frozen broccoli spears

2 cups carrots, thinly sliced

¼ teaspoon lemon pepper

½ teaspoon salt

1 lemon

1 cup sour cream

Melt butter in a frying pan. Add onions and sauté until tender. Add cauliflower, broccoli spears, and carrots. Cook until vegetables are tender crisp. Sprinkle with lemon pepper and salt. Cut lemon in half. Juice one lemon half and pour juice over vegetables. Slice other half and use for garnish. Arrange hot vegetables on a platter and dot with sour cream.
Yield: 12 servings.

Waldorf Salad

I N G R E D I E N T S

1 cup red apple chunks

1 cup green apple chunks

1 cup cantaloupe chunks or strawberries

1 cup celery, sliced

1 cup walnut pieces

2 tablespoons fresh mint, finely chopped

½ teaspoon ground ginger

1 cup mayonnaise

Combine all ingredients, mixing lightly. Chill.
Yield: 6 to 8 servings.

Snowflake Biscuits

INGREDIENTS

1 package dry yeast
½ cup warm water
5 cups flour
3 tablespoons sugar
1 tablespoon baking powder
1 teaspoon baking soda
1 teaspoon salt
¾ cup plus 2 tablespoons shortening
2 cups buttermilk

This recipe can be kept one week in the refrigerator and can be used as needed. The yeast makes these biscuits taste like rolls. Dissolve yeast in warm water. Let stand 10 minutes. Sift flour, sugar, baking powder, baking soda, and salt into a large bowl. Cut in the shortening. Stir in buttermilk and dissolved yeast. Work only until well moistened. Put in large, covered plastic container and refrigerate to use as needed. Take out only as much as needed; carefully roll on a well-floured surface ½-inch to ¾-inch thick. Cut with 2½-inch biscuit cutter. Bake at 400 degrees for 15 minutes.

Yield: 4 dozen biscuits.

Tip: Roll out and cut biscuits. Place on cookie sheet and freeze. When frozen, place in bag or container for freezing. (Will not stick together when frozen.) When ready to use take out what you need and allow 30 minutes at room temperature to thaw and then bake.

Sour Cream Banana Cake

INGREDIENTS

¼ cup butter

1⅓ cups sugar

2 eggs

1 teaspoon vanilla

2 cups flour

1 teaspoon baking powder

1 teaspoon baking soda

¾ teaspoon salt

1 cup sour cream

1 cup mashed ripe bananas

½ cup chopped nuts

Preheat oven to 350 degrees. Cream butter. Gradually add sugar and beat until light and fluffy. Beat in eggs. Add vanilla. Combine dry ingredients; add to creamed mixture alternately with sour cream. Add bananas and nuts; mix just until blended. Bake in greased and floured 9x13-inch pan for 35 to 40 minutes. Frost with Quick Caramel Frosting (recipe on next page).

Quick Caramel Frosting

½ cup butter
½ cup brown sugar
¼ cup evaporated milk
2¼ cups powdered sugar
1 teaspoon vanilla

Heat butter and brown sugar over low heat until sugar melts. Blend in evaporated milk; cool. Gradually beat in sugar until spreading consistency; add vanilla.

Talent Showcase

Everyone has special talents and abilities that are uniquely their own. Give family and friends a chance to share their talents with others at a gala dinner where they are the featured entertainment.

IDEAS

• Send out invitations for a dinner party and talent showcase. Explain in the invitations that there will be an admission of at least one entertainment selection per couple or family (or they could join with someone else). There are many kinds of talents—some are musical, others are artistic like painting, sewing, or scrapbooking. One talent may be writing a story while another is reading poetry. Cooking is a talent as well as woodworking and growing a beautiful garden. Encourage all your guests to participate. If need be, suggest things you know they do well.

• Since this will be a special evening, party attire will create a festive mood.

• A beautiful table will also evoke a sense of anticipation. Pull out all the stops and use your best to set the table. A simple flower arrangement, real or silk, will add the finishing touch.

• As your guests arrive, serve them Warmed Buttered Tomato Appetizer.

• Leisurely enjoy dinner surrounded by soft music, glowing candles, and the company of outstanding guests.

• Serve dessert during or after the talent showcase.

What lies behind us and what lies before us are small matters compared to what lies within us.

—Ralph Waldo Emerson

Menu

Warm Buttered Tomato Appetizer

Swiss Steak With Gravy

Mashed Potatoes

Fresh Buttered Asparagus

Salad de Maison

Snappy Rolls

Freezer Strawberry Jam

Chocolate Decadence with Sweet Cream

Warm Buttered Tomato Appetizer

INGREDIENTS

1 quart tomato juice

1 teaspoon Worcestershire sauce

¼ teaspoon salt

¼ teaspoon oregano

½ teaspoon marjoram

3 whole cloves

¼ cup butter or margarine

2 to 3 tablespoons lemon juice

Combine all ingredients. Heat, but do not boil. Remove cloves. Serve.

Swiss Steak and Gravy

INGREDIENTS

9 to 10 cubed steaks

Flour to coat

Butter

1 onion, chopped

2 cans (10¾ ounces each) cream of mushroom soup,
mixed with 2 soup cans water

Place flour in a large plastic bag. Add cubed steaks, one at a time, and shake to coat meat. Brown in a little butter. Place meat in a large, greased, oblong pan; cover with onion and pour soup mixture over all. Cover pan with foil and bake at 275 degrees for 3 hours. Serve with mashed potatoes.

Yield: 9 to 10 servings.

Tip: Turkey steaks or chicken breasts can be substituted for the cubed steak.

Salad de Maison

INGREDIENTS

2 bags of hearts of Romaine lettuce or 2 heads of Romaine lettuce, rinsed

1 carton cherry tomatoes, cut in half or 1 carton grape tomatoes

¾ cup shredded Parmesan Cheese

8 ounces shredded Swiss cheese

1 package center cut bacon, cooked and chopped

1 cup seasoned croutons

1 package (4 ounces) slivered almonds, toasted

Dressing (recipe follows)

Combine all salad ingredients in a large bowl. Just before serving, toss with dressing.

Salad de Maison Dressing

I N G R E D I E N T S
¾ cup oil
Juice of 1 lemon
2 to 3 cloves of garlic, crushed
or 1 teaspoon chopped garlic
¼ to ½ teaspoon salt
¼ teaspoon pepper

Combine all ingredients, mixing well, and chill overnight.

Snappy Rolls

I N G R E D I E N T S

2 cups self-rising flour
4 tablespoons mayonnaise
1 cup milk
1 teaspoon sugar

Preheat oven to 425 degrees. Combine all ingredients together in a medium bowl and mix well. Spoon into 12 lightly greased muffin cups. Bake for 16 to 18 minutes.

Tip: Best served warm the day of baking.

Freezer Strawberry Jam

INGREDIENTS

1 quart ripe strawberries, mashed

4 cups sugar (do not reduce sugar)

¾ cup water

1 box fruit pectin

Plastic storage containers

Place mashed strawberries into large bowl. Stir in sugar. Let stand 10 minutes, stirring occasionally. Bring water and pectin to a boil in small saucepan on high heat, stirring constantly. Continue boiling and stirring for 1 minute. Add to fruit mixture in bowl. Stir 3 minutes or until sugar is completely dissolved. Fill containers quickly to within ½-inch of tops; cover with lids. Let stand at room temperature 24 hours. Jam is ready to use. Refrigerate up to 3 weeks or freeze up to 1 year; thaw in refrigerator.

Yield: 6 cups.

Chocolate Decadence

INGREDIENTS

2 cups (12 ounces package) semisweet chocolate chips, divided

¾ cup butter, softened

¾ cup sugar

2 large eggs

1 cup flour

¼ cup milk

Sweetened cream (recipe follows)

Microwave 1 cup chips in medium, microwave safe bowl on high for 1 minute; stir. Microwave an additional 10 to 20 second intervals, stirring until smooth. Cool to room temperature. Preheat oven to 350 degrees. Line 9-inch round baking pan with foil. Lightly grease. Beat butter and sugar in large mixer bowl until creamy. Add eggs; beat on high speed for 2 to 3 minutes. Beat in melted chocolate. Gradually beat in flour alternately with milk. Stir in remaining chips. Spoon into prepared baking pan. Bake for 40 to 45 minutes until wooden pick inserted in center comes out slightly sticky. Cool completely in pan on wire rack. Lift cake from pan; remove foil. Cut into slices. Top each slice with sweetened cream and a few berries, such as raspberries, blueberries, blackberries, or sliced strawberries.

Yield: 12 servings.

Tip: Try adding 2 to 3 drops peppermint extract to batter before it is baked.

Sweet Cream

1 cup heavy whipping cream
2 tablespoons powdered sugar
½ teaspoon vanilla extract

Combine all ingredients in a small mixer bowl and beat until soft peaks form.

CELEBRATE SUNNY DAYS

April

Teach us to delight in simple things. —Rudyard Kipling

A Day at the Park

Catch a case of Spring Fever. The symptoms are most agreeable—no sniffles, chills or aches, just pure anticipation of the season's delights. The cure for Spring Fever is to spend a day at the park. Gather your family, relatives, friends or neighbors, and head out. The activities and food should be simple—after all, the goal is for everyone to enjoy themselves. These ideas are guaranteed to jump start a warm sunny spring day and get kids of all ages playing and laughing.

IDEAS

The park, with its wide open spaces is ideal for games and activities that require a lot of room, like the following:

• Peas in a Pod: This is "Hide and Seek" with a twist. One player hides while the others count to 100. Players then search for the player in hiding, joining him in the secret place until all but one have disappeared. (The trick is to keep from giggling when you're all behind a tree.) The last person to find the group becomes "it" next time.

• Tiger Tail: Several players line up, each holding the waist of the person in front of him. A "tail" (a bandanna or sock) is put in the back pocket of the last person in line. The object is for the first one in the line to snatch the tail. During the chase, no bonds within the tiger may be broken, even though some sections may be stretched beyond recognition. After a successful catch, the first person goes to the end of the line, and the game begins again.

• Human Maze: Any number of players can try this test of flexibility. One player (the "detangler") leaves while the rest join hands in a circle and, without letting go, step over and duck under each other's arms forming themselves into a knot, with heads, arms, and feet protruding in different directions. The "detangler" returns and tries to unravel the knot without loosing any hands.

• The Creature: This "creature" is formed when any number of players join hands in a circle. The "creature" tries to perform assigned tasks ducking under a fence or moving a piece of lawn furniture. Despite the trials the "creature" may face, this circle may not be broken.

• Bubble Magic: Make your own bubbles by combining three tablespoons glycerin (available at drug stores), ¾ cup Joy dishwashing soap, and a gallon of water (distilled water or tap water left out overnight works best). Search your home for waterproof, non-breakable items in unusual shapes. Cookie cutters, funnels, straws, or coat hangers twisted into any desired shape. Just dip the object into the bubble mixture and sweep it through the air.

• Tie apples with ribbon or thin rope and hang at various heights from a tree branch.

Did you know . . .

Americans consume an estimated 198 sandwiches per person a year, or more than forty-five billion total. By the time a student finishes high school, she is likely to have eaten 1,500 peanut butter and jelly sandwiches.

Menu

Your Favorite Sandwiches
Bite-sized Fruit in Ice Cream Cones
(Grapes, Melons, Strawberries)
Carrot and Celery Strips
Homemade Oreos
Sunshine Punch

Homemade Oreos

1 chocolate cake mix
2 eggs
½ cup butter, melted
4 ounces cream cheese
4 tablespoons butter, softened
2 cups powdered sugar

Preheat oven to 350 degrees. Mix cake mix, eggs, and butter. Roll into small balls and place on a cookie sheet. Bake for 9 minutes. Cool. Combine cream cheese, butter, and powdered sugar and mix until creamy. Frost cookies.

Sunshine Punch

INGREDIENTS
1 package lemon lime powdered drink mix
1 cup sugar
6 cups water
2 cans (12 ounces each) lemonade concentrate
2 cups pineapple juice
2 bottles (22 ounces each) ginger ale, chilled
A few drops of green food coloring

Dissolve powdered drink mix and sugar in water. Add lemonade concentrate and pineapple juice, chill. Before serving, add ginger ale and food coloring. Serve over ice.
Yield: 16 servings.

Backyard Olympics

Every two years the world comes together through the excitement and inspiration of the Olympic Games. Welcome spring and sunny weather by staging your own backyard Olympics. Although this is a perfect party for teens, any age can join in.

IDEAS

• Dust off the croquet set, set up a net for volleyball and badminton, construct an obstacle course, pump up the basketball and find the Frisbees. Borrow games and equipment from friends or neighbors if desired.

• Fashion gold, silver, and bronze medals from shiny metallic cardboard and ribbon to award to the winners in each event. Teenagers or children can help with this a few days before the event.

• To make the event even more fun, ask each teen to bring a new T-shirt, and you provide the fabric paints for him to make an Olympic shirt of his own design.

• After dinner when the evening settles in, divide your group into two teams for a game of flashlight tag. One team tries to tiptoe across the lawn while the other team tries to spot them and hit them with a flashlight beam. Anyone caught in this manner is out. After everyone either has been caught, or made it to the finish line, the teams reverse roles. The team that gets the most players to the finish line wins.

Let us remember everything, for it is the simplest joys that can bring the heart its greatest pleasure.

—Unknown

Menu

Gram's Sloppy Joes
Shell-Roni Salad
Cole Slaw
Chewy Fudge Brownies
Banana Slush

Gram's Sloppy Joes

INGREDIENTS
1 pound hamburger, browned
1 onion, chopped and browned with hamburger
1 tablespoon prepared mustard
1 can chicken gumbo soup
1 small can tomato sauce
½ cup ketchup
1 teaspoon Worcestershire sauce
Salt and pepper to taste
Hamburger buns

Simmer all ingredients until thickened. Serve on hamburger buns.
Yield: 4 to 6 servings.

Shell-Roni Salad

2 cups shell-roni pasta
1 small can corn, drained
1 small can beets, drained (optional)
1 half cucumber, peeled and diced
1 tablespoon chopped green onion
½ cup cubed cheese
Mayonnaise

Cook the pasta, rinse with cold water, drain. Combine the pasta, corn, beets, cucumber, onion, and cheese in a large bowl. Add enough mayonnaise to generously moisten the salad. Yield: 4 to 6 servings.

Coleslaw

INGREDIENTS
1 head (about 3 pounds) cabbage, finely chopped or grated
¼ cup finely diced carrots
½ cup sugar
1 teaspoon salt
½ cup sour cream
½ cup salad dressing
2 tablespoons white vinegar
2 tablespoons vegetable oil

Combine cabbage, carrots, sugar and salt; set aside. In another container mix sour cream, salad dressing, vinegar, and vegetable oil. Pour over cabbage mixture and toss well. Chill at least one hour before serving.

Chewy Fudge Brownies

INGREDIENTS

1 package butter fudge cake mix

2 eggs

½ cup melted butter

1 cup miniature marshmallows

1 cup coarsely chopped walnuts (optional)

Preheat oven to 350 degrees. Grease a 9x13-inch pan. Combine cake mix, eggs, and butter; mix well. Batter will be stiff. Stir in marshmallows and walnuts; spread in prepared pan. Bake for 20 to 30 minutes or until set. Frost with favorite fudge icing.

Banana Slush

INGREDIENTS

1 can (6 ounces) frozen orange juice

1 can (6 ounces) frozen lemonade

1 can (46 ounces) pineapple juice

5 large bananas, mashed

6 cups water

3 cups sugar

Lemon lime carbonated beverage or ginger ale

In a large saucepan cook water and sugar together until mixture forms a syrup. Mix fruit juices together; add sugar syrup. Stir well. Pour into family-sized freezer containers and freeze. Thaw slightly and mix well with lemon lime carbonated beverage or ginger ale.

CELEBRATE NEW BEGINNINGS

May

Love is the sharing of songs and of silences, and the holding of memories only the heart can see.

—Unknown

Something Borrowed, Something Blue . . .

According to folklore, the first bridal shower was given in Holland. A young Dutch man, who was known to all as generous and benevolent to the poor, found himself in need as he planned to marry. In return for his kindness, his friends and neighbors "showered" the bride and groom with gifts. Bridal Showers in America were originally given during quilting bees when women worked on a bridal bedcover for the couple.

IDEAS

• Establish a gentle ambience with a centerpiece of glowing white candles in various sized clear glass cylinders wrapped with white lace.

• Nestle the candles on a white or pink tablecloth. Accent with gardenias or camellias floating in shallow clear glass bowls. (Different white flowers could also be used.)

• Fasten large white bows and white silk or fresh flowers to the back of each chair around the table.

• Freeze orange blossoms in the ice cubes.

• Float more gardenias and camellias and candles in the bathtub of the guest bathroom.

• Small ornate purses can serve as place card holders, napkin holders, and as favors. Tuck a small bouquet of lavender into each purse with a note explaining this tradition: In England during the Victorian age, lavender was used to perfume bridal hope chests.

• After lunch, present a "fashion show" with girls of various ages modeling the bride's favorite dresses she wore growing up.

Did you know . . .

As far as we can tell from recorded history, the wearing of white wedding dresses dates back to royal marriages in the 1600s. Pure white cloth was expensive to obtain for most brides, so, before the 1800s, many brides wore pink. White wedding gowns were popularized by Queen Victoria when she wedded Alfred. A borrowed veil is believed to be good luck because in Victorian times veils were costly and considered a prized possession.

Bridal Bouquets grew out of the small bouquets (nosegays) that ladies carried at dances beginning in the mid 1800s.

The first types of wedding cakes made in America were known as "great cakes" and were variations on fruit, nut, and spice cakes from old British recipes. Sometimes women would bake wedding cakes before finding a bridegroom as a demonstration of their culinary abilities. Until the nineteenth century, pieces of wedding cake were crumbled over the bride and groom. As finely ground flour, baking powder, and baking soda became available just prior to the Civil War, the white wedding cake became popular.

Menu

Salmon Pasta Salad
Lemon Crowned Blueberry Muffins
Papaya Slices and Raspberries with Lime Wedges
Chocolate Truffle Torte
Sparkling Citrus Cooler

Salmon Pasta Salad

1 pound fresh or frozen salmon, poached and chunked
1 package (12 ounces) fettuccine, cooked and rinsed
1 pound fresh spinach, rinsed and cut into strips
½ cup slivered almonds
½ cup sliced green onions
4 ounces grated Parmesan cheese
2 tablespoons chopped parsley
Dressing (recipe follows)

Combine all salad ingredients in a large bowl.

Pasta Salad Dressing

INGREDIENTS

2 eggs

1 tablespoon white vinegar

1/3 cup vegetable oil

1 tablespoon sweet basil

2 teaspoons crushed rosemary

1½ teaspoons dry mustard

1 teaspoon salt

1 teaspoon dill weed

1 teaspoon grated lemon peel

½ teaspoon ground pepper

¼ teaspoon tarragon

To prepare dressing; whip eggs in blender jar. Add vinegar, lemon, and sugar. With blender running, drizzle oil into egg mixture. Blend in remaining dressing ingredients. Pour over salad and toss to coat. Chill.

Yield: 8 to 10 servings.

Lemon Crowned Blueberry Muffins

INGREDIENTS
1¾ cup flour
½ cup sugar
2½ teaspoons baking powder
¾ teaspoon salt
¾ cup milk
⅓ cup vegetable oil
1 egg, beaten
1 cup fresh blueberries
2 tablespoons sugar
2 teaspoons grated lemon rind

Topping
2 tablespoons melted butter
¾ teaspoon lemon juice
Sugar

In a large bowl, combine flour, sugar, baking powder, and salt. Make a well in center of mixture. Combine milk, oil, and egg; add to dry ingredients in well; stir until moistened. Toss blueberries with 2 tablespoons sugar and lemon rind. Fold into batter. Fill muffin papers or greased muffin pans about two-thirds full. Bake at 400 degrees for 20 minutes, or until golden brown. While muffins bake, prepare topping by mixing melted butter and lemon juice. Dip tops of warm muffins in butter mixture, then in sugar.
Yield: 12 to 18 muffins.

Chocolate Truffle Torte

INGREDIENTS

1 package chocolate cake mix
1 package (4½ ounces) chocolate instant pudding
⅓ cup milk
2 cups chilled whipping cream
½ teaspoon vanilla
Nuts for garnish (optional)

Bake cake as directed in two round layers. Cool. Split cake to make four layers. Blend pudding mix and milk in a large bowl; stir until mix is dissolved. Add whipping cream and vanilla; beat until mixture is just stiff enough to spread. Spread between layers and on top with pudding mix. Garnish with nuts. Refrigerate.

Yield: 12 servings.

Sparkling Citrus Cooler

I N G R E D I E N T S
1 bottle (48 ounces) lime flavored sparkling water, chilled
1 can (12 ounces) frozen lemonade concentrate, thawed
¼ cup fresh lime juice
8 lime slices or wedges, if desired

In a 2-quart, nonmetallic pitcher, combine sparkling water, lemonade concentrate, and lime juice; mix well. Immediately serve in glasses over ice. Garnish each with lime slice. Yield: 8 (1 cup) servings.

Life is a series of new beginnings and we are unaware
of what sweet miracles may come.

—Unknown

Garden Patio Gathering

Whether your garden covers an entire backyard, a deck, or merely a small window ledge, May is a great time to invite friends over to celebrate the joy of watching things grow.

IDEAS

• Combine coordinating patterns and fabrics for the tablecloth, such as floral patterns, pastels, stripes, and lace. Colorful bed sheets or quilts that you have on hand make inexpensive substitutes for tablecloths.

• Use the beautifully presented food as the centerpiece.

• Wherever possible, use garden utensils to serve the food and beverage.

Use a large new, cleaned plastic or clay flowerpot lined with lettuce leaves for the salad and a plastic trowel to serve it.

Serve the fruit in a red leaf lettuce lined clean clay flower pot saucer and place the dip in a small plastic flowerpot centered in the middle of the fruit.

Use a plastic watering can to pour the beverage.

• For a fun game, try a gardening gift exchange. Ask each guest to bring a small wrapped gift related to gardening. (A packet of seeds, a pot, a pair of gardening gloves, etc.) Number pieces of paper corresponding to the number of guests in attendance. Have each guest draw a piece of paper from a clay pot. The person who draws number one gets to choose which gift they want to open. When they've opened it, the person who chooses number two can either pick a gift of their own—or take the gift that number one opened. It keeps going until everyone has had a choice of either an opened, or a wrapped gift. When the party is over, each guest will leave with a little gift, and a little inspiration for her own garden.

• At the end of the party, have each guest plant an herb pot as a favor. Supply terra-cotta pots and saucers, potting soil, and a variety of small herb plants. Popsicle sticks can be used as herb markers.

Menu

Pasta Chicken Caesar Salad

Homegrown Bread

Herb Butter

Fresh Fruit Bowl with Orange Coconut Dip

Pineapple Angel Food Cake

Party Waters

White Grape Cooler

Pasta Chicken Caesar Salad

I N G R E D I E N T S
1 large head Romaine lettuce, washed and dried
1 package (8 ounces) Penne pasta, cooked and rinsed with cold water
3 chicken breasts, grilled and cubed
Bottled Caesar salad dressing
Freshly grated Parmesan cheese
Herbed croutons

Tear lettuce into bite sized pieces and place in salad bowl; cover and refrigerate. Just before serving, combine the lettuce, chicken, and cooked pasta; toss with enough salad dressing to coat, and top with Parmesan cheese and croutons. Serve immediately.
Yield: 6 servings.

Homegrown Bread

INGREDIENTS
2 clay flowerpots (4-inch), washed and dried well
Unsalted butter
1 loaf frozen bread dough, thawed

Season pots by rubbing butter on the inside of the pots. Heat pots in 375 degree oven for 30 minutes. Cut bread dough in half; place each half, cut side down, in a prepared pot. Cover and let rise in a warm place until doubled in bulk. Bake at 375 degrees for 30 to 35 minutes. Remove from oven and let bread cool in pots for 5 minutes. Remove bread from pots and finish cooling on a wire rack. Wash and dry clay pots in which the bread was baked. Line each with a patterned napkin or fabric square and return the bread to the pot. Tie miniature garden tools to the side of the pot with ribbon.

HERB BUTTERS
Try these instead of plain butter. For each flavored butter, either combine the ingredients in the bowl of a food processor until smooth, or cream them together by hand in a small bowl. Cover and refrigerate until ready to use. Use a melon baller, if you like, to make perfect spheres of the butter before chilling.

DILL BUTTER
8 tablespoons sweet butter, 3 tablespoons chopped fresh dill.

HERB BUTTER
8 tablespoons sweet butter, 1 tablespoon finely chopped fresh herb of your choice.

Orange Coconut Dip

I N G R E D I E N T S
1 package (8 ounces) cream cheese, softened
¼ cup frozen orange juice concentrate
1 cup whipping cream
1/3 cup coconut
2 tablespoons chopped pecans

Combine cream cheese and orange juice concentrate. Stir until smooth. Whip cream. Fold whipped cream, coconut and nuts into cream cheese mixture. Keep refrigerated until ready for use. Serve with fresh fruit.

Yield: 3 cups

Pineapple Angel Food Cake

INGREDIENTS

¾ cup sugar

2½ tablespoons cornstarch

⅛ teaspoon salt

¼ cup lemon juice

3 egg yolks, slightly beaten

½ cup pineapple juice

2 tablespoons butter

1 pint whipping cream, whipped and sweetened

One large angel food cake

Mix all ingredients, except cream and cake, and cook until thick at a low temperature, stirring constantly. Cut cake into 4 layers. On first layer put filling, on second layer put whipping cream, on third layer put filling. Top with remaining layer and cover entire cake with sweetened whipping cream.

Party Waters

Pretty and refreshing. You'll be amazed at the flavors that pop out when you soak fresh fruits, tender herbs, and edible blossoms in clear glass pitchers of icy water. Just combine the cleaned ingredients, add water, and cover and chill for 1 to 2 hours. Slide the ice into the pitchers and pour into pretty glasses to serve.

HERE ARE A FEW IDEAS:

LEMON HERB WATER

Lemon slices, mint or basil leaves, and blooming, pesticide-free, yellow roses

LIME CUCUMBER WATER

Lime slices, matchstick cucumber slices, and mint leaves

BERRY ROSE WATER

Raspberries and blooming, pesticide-free, pink roses

ORANGE WATER

Orange and kumquat slices, and pesticide-free nasturtiums

White Grape Cooler

1 can (12 ounces) frozen apple juice concentrate, thawed
1 can (11½ ounces) frozen white grape juice concentrate, thawed
3 cups cold water
6 cups (about 1½ liters) lemon lime soda pop (can use diet)
Lemon and lime slices

Mix juice concentrates in large container. Stir in water. Just before serving, add soda pop and lemon and lime slices. Pour over ice in glasses.

Yield: 12 servings.

CELEBRATE SUMMER

June

If a summer night could talk, it would probably boast that it invented romance. —Bern Williams

School's Out

There's so much to love about summer. Days filled with swimming at the pool, bike rides, and picnics. Nights spent listening for the ice cream truck bell and, occasionally, allowing the children to stay up an hour later to finish a game of tag. Summer spreads sunshine throughout our lives and the lives of everyone around us. It makes us smile and giggle. It's a perfect time for a School's Out party. Invite family and friends to join your celebration.

IDEAS

Set up tables around the backyard for activity stations. Tape paper onto the tops of the tables for protection. Have everyone rotate between all the activities. Some activity stations could include:

• Take home containers, made by having each person decorate his own sack.

• Supply one of the tables with clay pot painting supplies. Add a bit of soil to the pot, sprinkle in some grass seed, and watch the grass grow.

• Have a cupcake, or cookie, decorating booth.

• On a patio, or cemented area, draw a hopscotch with chalk and give instructions on the finer points of the game.

• Make candy skewers by placing a variety of soft candies on wooden skewers. Candies that work well are large gumdrops, gummy worms, frogs, and fruits, marshmallows, candy fruit slices, and soft nonpareil candy. Use your imagination. Place the finished product in a plastic bag and secure with a ribbon.

• One area of the lawn could hold a "fishing" pond and a ring toss game.

• Use a larger table as a snack station. Feature items from the menu.

Rest is not idleness, and to lie sometimes on the grass on a summer day listening to the murmur of water, or watching the clouds float across the sky, is hardly a waste of time. —John Lubbock

Menu

Soft and Simple Pretzels
Apple Slices, Grapes and Banana Chunks
Commercial Caramel Fruit Dip
Gooey Goodies

Soft and Simple Pretzels

INGREDIENTS

1 package (2 pounds) frozen bread dough rolls

2 tablespoons salt

2 quarts boiling water

1 egg white, slightly beaten

Sesame, caraway, or poppy seeds or coarse salt

Defrost frozen rolls in the refrigerator overnight, or at room temperature for 30 minutes. Shape each roll into a 12-inch strip. Twist each strip into a pretzel shape. Let rise, uncovered, 30 to 45 minutes. Dissolve salt in boiling water. Lower 3 to 5 pretzels into the boiling water. Boil 2 minutes, turning once. Remove with slotted spoon to a paper towel. Place boiled pretzels on a greased baking sheet and brush with egg white. Sprinkle with desired seeds or salt. Bake at 350 degrees for 20 to 25 minutes or until golden brown.

Yield: 3 dozen pretzels.

Gooey Goodies

INGREDIENTS
1 package (18 ounces) Golden Grahams cereal
1 package (15.6 ounces) Rice Chex Cereal (reserve about 2 to 3 cups for another use)
2 cups coconut
1 can cashews (optional)
1½ cups butter
2 cups sugar
2 cups light corn syrup

Mix the cereal, coconut and cashews in a *very* large bowl. Combine butter, sugar, and corn syrup in a saucepan; bring to a boil. Boil 2 to 3 minutes. Pour syrup, a little at a time, onto the cereal mixture, and stir to mix. Continue to pour and stir until syrup and cereal are combined. Mixture should be gooey. Spoon onto waxed paper to cool. Store in an airtight container.

A Midsummer's Night Rendezvous

The evening of the longest day of the year, the summer solstice, is deemed as Midsummer's Night. As legend has it, on that evening, the veil is thin between reality and fantasy. Fairies always come out on Midsummer's Night and leave a ring behind where they've danced. It is said that a girl who gathers seven wildflowers and places them on her pillow on Midsummer's Night, will dream of the man she will marry. This balmy, starry summer night just begs for a moonlight celebration.

IDEAS

• Turn your backyard into a magical setting. Line the walkway leading to the party with luminaries or tiki torches. String miniature Christmas lights all over the sides of a deck. Wrap wire around the lips of clear glass jars, making a handle to hang the jars from tree branches. Place white votive candles in each jar and light them just before the party begins. Tuck a few citronella candles around to ward off bugs.

• Use a lavender or medium green tablecloth. Cluster white pillar candles in the center of the table. This will serve as a buffet table.

• For an easy centerpiece, purchase a 12 or 14 inch square of wheat grass from a health food market and place it in a plastic lined basket, trimming as necessary. Cut small slits in the grass to "plant" small flowers like pansies, violas, etc. Nestle in the flowers and wow your guests. Real grass can be grown by using the instructions in the recipe section of this party.

• Instead of a heavy meal, present small bowls of soup and a variety of appetizers. This sampling of appetizers is known as tapas. Tapas is a wonderful Spanish custom that Americans are coming to enjoy.

Conversation and delicious food go hand in hand in Spain, so most Spaniards gather for a chat over an array of small appetizers before both lunch and dinner. The dishes can range from simple to sophisticated. The ones suggested here are easy to do and most can be prepared ahead of time.

• Relax, enjoy the company, take in all the splendor of the evening—and be sure to watch for fairies.

Menu

Bacon Shrimp Bites

Skewers

Sassy Cheese

Can-opener Salsa with Chips

Tortilla Soup

Strawberry Gazpacho

Chocolate Madeleines

Low-Voltage Pina Coladas

Bacon Shrimp Bites

INGREDIENTS
40 large ready-to-eat shrimp, peeled, tails intact
20 bacon slices, cut in half
2 tablespoons finely chopped fresh basil
2 tablespoons finely chopped fresh thyme

Cook bacon slices until soft and pliable. Wrap each shrimp with a slightly cooked bacon piece, securing with a wooden pick. Combine basil and thyme; sprinkle 2 tablespoons of herb mixture onto shrimp bites. Place on a lightly greased rack in a broiler pan. Broil 6 inches from heat (with oven door partially open) for a few minutes on each side or until bacon is crisp. Sprinkle with remaining 2 tablespoons herbs.

Yield: 40 appetizers.

Tip: These can be prepared ahead of time, refrigerated, and warmed before serving. Sprinkle with remaining herbs just before serving.

Skewers

I N G R E D I E N T S

On 6-inch bamboo skewers, spear of any of these suggested combinations:

- shrimp and green grapes
- melon and smoked turkey
- apple chunks and ham
- chicken cubes and avocado
- cherry tomatoes and roast beef cubes marinated in vinaigrette dressing
- Swiss cheese cubes, ham cubes and a pickle
- your favorite combinations

The skewers look especially dazzling when placed standing up into a heavy cabbage head.

Sassy Cheese

INGREDIENTS
1 package (8 ounces) cream cheese
1 bottle raspberry-jalapeno sauce
(Found by the barbecue sauce in grocery stores or specialty kitchen shops.)
1 box snack crackers

Place cream cheese on a serving plate. Drizzle with sauce and serve with crackers.

Can-opener Salsa

INGREDIENTS

1 can petite diced tomatoes

1 can petite diced tomatoes with jalapenos

½ small onion, chopped or grated

1 can corn with juice

1 can kidney beans, drained

1 can black beans, drained

1 package Italian dressing mix

1 teaspoon sugar

1 to 2 tablespoons vinegar

1 avocado, chopped

Combine all ingredients except avocado. Chill. Just before serving, add avocado. Serve with chips. Refrigerate any leftovers in an airtight container.

Tortilla Soup #1

3 tablespoons butter
1 tablespoon olive oil
1 cup chopped onion
4 tablespoons flour
2 cartons (32 ounces each) chicken broth
1 package (1.25 ounces) mild taco seasoning mix
1 can corn, drained
1 can kidney beans, drained
1 pound chicken breasts, cooked and shredded
(canned chicken can be substituted)

Garnishes:
Shredded Monterey Jack cheese
Sour cream
Avocado, diced
Broken tortilla chips
Fresh cilantro, chopped

Sauté onion in butter and olive oil. Add flour, and mix well. Add remaining ingredients, and bring to a boil. Reduce heat and simmer, uncovered, 30 minutes. To serve, place a small amount of chicken in each bowl and add soup. Top with garnishes.

Yield: 6 servings.

Tip: For a thicker soup add an additional 1 to 2 tablespoons flour, mixed with a little cold water during the last five minutes of cooking.

Tortilla Soup #2

INGREDIENTS

5 boneless, skinless chicken breasts cut into bite-sized pieces
1 bottle (4 pounds) mild picante sauce
1 box (32 ounces) chicken broth
2 cans (11 ounces each) corn, drained
2 cans (15.25 ounces each) red kidney beans, drained

Garnishes:
Grated cheese
Broken tortilla chips
Black olive slices
Sour cream
Sprig of cilantro

In a large pot, cook the chicken in the picante sauce on medium heat for 20 to 30 minutes. Add chicken broth, corn, and beans. To serve, ladle soup into bowls and top with any or all of the garnishes listed above.
Yield: 10 to 12 servings.

Strawberry Gazpacho

INGREDIENTS

2 quarts strawberries, rinsed, hulled, and halved

1 ripe mango, pitted, peeled, and diced

2 kiwis, peeled and diced

¼ cup sugar, or sugar to taste

1 cup white grape juice

3 tablespoons fresh lime juice

½ cup vanilla low fat yogurt

Dice one cup strawberries; combine in a small bowl with mango and kiwi. Reserve and refrigerate ½ cup. Puree remaining halved strawberries with the sugar in food processor until smooth. Pour into a bowl; stir in grape juice, lime juice, and remaining diced fruit. Refrigerate at least two hours, or up to one day. To serve, ladle gazpacho into individual bowls. Top with yogurt and reserved fruit.

Chocolate Madeleines

INGREDIENTS

1¼ cups flour

1 cup sugar

⅛ teaspoon salt

¾ cup butter, melted

5 tablespoons unsweetened cocoa

3 eggs

2 egg yolks

½ teaspoon vanilla

½ cup miniature chocolate chips, optional

Powdered sugar

Preheat oven to 350 degrees. Lightly coat a madeleine pan (see tip below) with vegetable spray. Combine flour, sugar, and salt in a medium saucepan. Combine melted butter and cocoa; stir into dry ingredients. Whip the eggs, egg yolks, and vanilla with a fork until well-blended; stir into chocolate mixture, blending well. Cook over low heat, stirring constantly, until mixture is barely warm; do not simmer or boil! Remove from heat and let cool a few minutes. Fold in chocolate chips, if desired. Fill each mold half full with batter, taking care not to overfill. Bake for 8 to 10 minutes, or until cake tester comes out clean. Invert onto wire rack; cool completely. Dust with powdered sugar. Store in an airtight container.

Yield: 32 cakes.

Tip: Madeleines are light spongy cakes that are eaten like cookies. To make these little cakes, batter is poured into greased madeleines pans. Each pan contains small molds shaped in the form of seashells with scalloped edges. As the batter bakes, it takes on the form of the shells. You can find madeleine pans in specialty housewares and kitchen stores. The number of molds per pan, the mold dimension, and the mold design vary by manufacturer. Because of this, you may get a different yield than the recipe. If you cannot find madeleine pans, a small amount of batter may be baked in greased miniature muffin pans. Bake at 350 degrees for 15 to 20 minutes.

Low-Voltage Pina Coladas

I N G R E D I E N T S
1 can (45 ounces) unsweetened pineapple juice
½ cup cream of coconut
1 bottle (10 ounces) lemon-lime soda
1 cup crushed ice
8 small pineapple chunks (optional)

Mix half of all ingredients in blender jar on medium speed for 30 seconds. Pour mixture into pitcher or punch bowl. Repeat with remaining ingredients. Pour into chilled glasses. Garnish each with a pineapple chunk.
Yield: 8 servings.

Real Grass

INGREDIENTS
Clay Pot
Plastic wrap
Soil
Grass seed
Water

Five to seven days will bring a velvety, thick stand of green grass. Pour soil into pot to a level of two inches below the top of the rim. Sprinkle a layer of grass seed over the soil. Pour a little water into the pot. Place a piece of plastic wrap loosely over the top of pot. Put pot in a sunny spot (not in direct sunlight). After one or two days, remove plastic wrap. Continue to water as needed.

CELEBRATE YOUR LEGACY

July

The Heritage of the past is the seed that brings forth the harvest of the future. —Etched in stone on the U.S. National Archives building in Washington, D.C.

Heritage Day

Our flag is a symbol of everything we cherish in the United States of America. As we salute its broad stripes and bright stars, it is there to remind us of our freedom and the struggles we have endured. It serves as a symbol of strength, reminding us to hold fast to the patriotic dreams of our forefathers. While we celebrate the birth of our great nation as Americans, we can also celebrate our legacy and the heritage that brought us here.

IDEAS

• Carry out a global theme from the beginning. Purchase a bag of small International flags from a party or craft store. Glue the flags to toothpicks, and use them as part of the decorations for the table and the food.

• Fly the U.S. flag during the party, whatever the date.

• Cover the table with any color of bulletin board paper, found at school supply stores and purchased by the yard. Glue travel brochures from various countries on it. You could also use markers to write the names of the countries on the paper. Let your imagination go.

• Hang a large map of the world and invite your guests to write their names on the countries of their ancestors.

• Ask every family or couple to bring a dish that reflects their family heritage. Have them tell about the food and any traditions behind it. Tell guests you, as the hostess, will provide the dessert. (It is a good idea to make sure there will be a main dish.)

• To create a centerpiece, ask each cook to send a copy of their recipe to you. Using white and medium blue papers make enough copies of each recipe for everyone, or every couple, in the group to have one. Compile the recipes into stacks (one of each recipe), roll them up lengthwise, tie them with red ribbon, slip an American flag under the ribbon, and stand them up in a large clear glass jar or bowl. Invite guests to take one as they leave the party.

• Several days before the party, make red, white, and blue "crackers." Cut an empty paper towel roll in half. Measure the length of the roll and cut tissue paper, light-weight craft paper, crepe paper, or other paper about six inches longer than the roll. Wrap the paper around the roll, leaving three inches of paper on each end of the roll (enough to cover the opening), and adhere in place. Fill the roll or "cracker" with small items such as taffy, coins, bracelets, trinkets from the dollar store, gum, toys, etc. Tie each end of the roll with ribbon so all of the contents are secure in the roll.

Fringe the ends of the paper if desired. Lay one by each place as you set the table.

• Just before serving, stand a sparkler on top of each dessert and light it.

• After dinner, ask everyone to tell the group which countries their ancestors came from and a little about them, such as what brought the family to America, when they came, and perhaps some family traditions that were passed down. (When you invite your guests explain what your plan is so they'll be prepared.)

Menu

Friends and Family Pot Luck
American Cheesecake
Stars and Stripes Fruit Pastry
Red, White, and Blue Parfaits

American Cheesecake

2 packages (8 ounces each) cream cheese, softened
$1/3$ cup sugar
2 tablespoons lemon juice
1 container (8 ounces) frozen whipped topping, thawed, divided
1 graham cracker crust
Strawberry halves and blueberries

Beat cream cheese, sugar, and lemon juice in large bowl with electric mixer on medium speed until well blended. Gently stir in 2 cups of the whipped topping. Spoon into crust. Refrigerate 3 hours, or until set. Spread remaining whipped topping over top. Arrange berries in rows to resemble the American flag.

Yield: 6 to 8 servings.

Stars and Stripes Fruit Pastry

INGREDIENTS

One half of a 17¼ ounces package frozen puff pastry (1 sheet)

2 cups sliced fresh strawberries

1½ cups fresh raspberries or blackberries

1 cup fresh blueberries

¼ cup sugar

Coarse sugar, red or blue sugar, granulated sugar, or powdered sugar

½ cup whipping cream

¼ cup sour cream

1 tablespoon sugar

Thaw the puff pastry according to the package directions. Chill a medium mixing bowl and beaters from an electric mixer. (A chilled bowl and beaters will help the cream to whip into peaks more quickly.) In a large mixing bowl, toss together the berries and the ¼ cup sugar. Set aside. On a lightly floured surface, unfold puff pastry. Using floured, star-shape cutters of different sizes, cut pastry into stars. Arrange star pastries on an ungreased baking sheet. Bake at 350 degrees for 15 minutes, or until golden. Remove from baking sheet; cool slightly on a wire rack. Brush stars lightly with water; sprinkle with coarse sugar, colored sugar, or powdered sugar. In the chilled bowl, combine whipping cream, sour cream, and 1 tablespoon sugar. Beat with the chilled beaters of the electric mixer on low speed until soft peaks form. To serve, arrange the berries and pastry stars on 6 serving plates. Pipe or spoon whipped cream onto plates.

Yield: 6 servings.

Red, White, and Blue Parfaits

INGREDIENTS

1⅓ cups whipping cream
1 container (8 ounces) sour cream
⅓ cup sifted powdered sugar
6 cups fresh raspberries, halved strawberries, or both
6 cups fresh blueberries

In a large mixing bowl, combine whipping cream, sour cream, and sifted powdered sugar. Beat with an electric mixer on medium speed until mixture thickens and holds soft peaks. Serve immediately, or cover and chill up to 24 hours. (Cream may thicken upon chilling. Stir before serving.) To serve, alternate layers of berries with whipped cream mixture in twelve 16-ounce glasses or bowls.

Yield: 12 servings.

Don't just count your years, make your years count!

-Ernest Meyers

It's Not My Birthday

Birthdays are a time to reflect on our lives and remember and give thanks to our parents, who gave us this precious gift. However, as each birthday passes by, so another year is added to our age. The best part about celebrating "It's Not My Birthday" is you can enjoy a full fledged birthday party, cake and presents included, but no one gets any older! You can't beat that!

IDEAS

• Create a festive mood with color—bright, fun color everywhere. Hang party hats, horns, and blowouts. Put lights everywhere.

• Carry the theme to the table and use a brightly colored tablecloth. Mix and match colored dishes, glasses, and napkins. Another idea: paper and plastic partyware comes in bright colors, is inexpensive and makes clean-up a breeze.

• Ask each guest to bring a wrapped "white elephant" gift to exchange.

• After dinner, play "Who Am I." Type a list of questions, leaving room for the answers. At the bottom of the page, leave a blank for the person's name. Pass a list to everyone and let them fill it out. As the hostess, you read the list of questions and answers, one by one, omitting the names. Let everyone guess who the person is. Some of the questions might be:

My favorite food to eat
A food I would never eat
My favorite color
My dream vacation would be
The chore that I dread is
My wildest fantasy is
My favorite book is
My favorite movie is

A good childhood memory I have is
My pet peeve is
My favorite food to cook is
I was born in
My favorite thing to do is

• As a party favor, partially dip fortune cookies (available at oriental markets) in milk chocolate, then roll in toffee bits (found by the chocolate chips in the grocery store). Send them home in small oriental take-out boxes.

Menu

Teriyaki Chicken
Or Sukiyaki
Oriental Salad
Ham Fried Rice
Candy Bar Cake
Pineapple Frost

Teriyaki Chicken

INGREDIENTS

1½ tablespoons brown sugar

1½ tablespoons sugar

⅔ cup soy sauce

½ cup lemon juice

2 cloves garlic

2 pounds bone-in chicken breasts, skinned

½ teaspoon grated ginger

Combine all ingredients except chicken. Add chicken and set aside for 30 minutes. Pour a little water in bottom of a broiler pan and place rack on top. Place chicken on rack. Bake for 1 hour at 350 degrees, or until done. Turn occasionally and brush with marinade.

Tip: Can be grilled on a barbecue.

Sukiyaki

INGREDIENTS

1 cup water
3 tablespoons sugar
4 tablespoons soy sauce, divided
1 Sirloin roast (2 to 3 pounds) thinly sliced and cut into strips
(a butcher can slice the meat)
3 to 4 carrots, sliced
3 to 4 celery ribs, sliced
Sugar water (3 tablespoons sugar to 1 cup water)
1 to 2 tablespoons cornstarch

Combine water and sugar in a large pan and bring to a boil; add 2 tablespoons soy sauce. Brown beef in this mixture for 5 to 10 minutes; add vegetables and cover with more sugar water and remaining 2 tablespoons soy sauce. Simmer 20 to 25 minutes. Thicken mixture by adding 1 to 2 tablespoons cornstarch (dissolved in a little cold water). Cook until sauce is thick. Serve over rice.

Yield: 4 to 6 servings.

Oriental Salad

INGREDIENTS

6 cups chopped romaine lettuce

2 cups chopped red cabbage

2 cups chopped Napa cabbage

1 cup shredded or julienned carrots

2 tablespoons sliced almonds

1 cup rice noodles

Toss the romaine lettuce with red cabbage, Napa cabbage, and carrots. Sprinkle almonds over salad and then add rice noodles. Serve with Oriental Dressing on the side (recipe on next page).

Oriental Dressing

INGREDIENTS
¾ cup honey
1 cup mayonnaise
2 teaspoons sesame oil
6 tablespoons rice wine vinegar
4 tablespoons Dijon mustard

Combine all the ingredients in a small bowl or shaker jar; blend or shake thoroughly. Refrigerate for several hours.

Ham Fried Rice

INGREDIENTS
2 tablespoons butter
2 ribs celery, diced
½ cup chopped onion
2 cups diced ham
6 cups refrigerated cooked rice
Soy sauce

Melt butter in a large frying pan; add vegetables and cook until tender, not brown. Add ham and rice; stir until blended. Add soy sauce until mixture is a light brown, or to taste. Heat thoroughly.
Yield: 6 to 8 servings.

Candy Bar Cake

I N G R E D I E N T S

6 to 7 Milky Way candy bars (14 ounces total)

1½ cup butter

1½ cup sugar

4 eggs, well beaten

2½ cups flour

¾ teaspoon baking soda

1¼ cup buttermilk

1 teaspoon vanilla

1½ cup pecans, chopped

Icing (recipe follows)

Preheat oven to 350 degrees. Melt Milky Way bars with ½ cup butter. Remove from heat, and cool. Cream remaining 1 cup butter with sugar. Add beaten eggs and cooled chocolate mixture. Sift flour with baking soda. Add flour alternately with buttermilk, blending well. Add vanilla and 1 cup nuts. Sprinkle ½ cup of finely chopped nuts in a greased Bundt pan. Pour cake batter over nuts. Bake for 50 to 60 minutes, or until pick inserted in center comes out clean. Cool in pan on rack for 30 minutes. Invert and remove from pan and cool completely. Yield: 12 to 16 servings.

Candy Bar Cake Icing

1¼ cups sugar
½ cup evaporated milk
¼ cup butter
½ cup marshmallow cream
½ cup chocolate chips
½ cup pecans, chopped

Combine sugar and evaporated milk. Cook to a soft ball stage. Remove from heat and add butter, marshmallow cream, and chocolate chips, stirring until all have melted. Add pecans. Drizzle over the top of the cake.

Pineapple Frost

3 cups pineapple sherbet, softened

2 cans (8 ounces each) crushed pineapple, drained

2 cups half and half

$2/3$ cup light corn syrup

Ginger ale

In a blender jar, combine sherbet, pineapple, half and half and corn syrup; blend until pineapple is very fine. Pour into bowl; cover and freeze. Before serving add ginger ale and stir to make a slush.

Yield: 12 servings.

August

No day is ordinary if you have made a memory. —Unknown

Come-As-You-Are Party

Tuesday is the most ordinary day of the week. It doesn't start the week or end it. It's not even in the middle. It is just plain ordinary. A dinner party is a perfect opportunity to turn a common Tuesday into a memorable celebration.

IDEAS

• Call your guests at various times of the day, and even different days of the week, and invite them to your dinner party. Inform your guest that the party attire is "Come As You Are When You're Called" and ask what he is wearing. He must wear this to the party.

• An outdoor area is ideal for the dinner. Set up a picnic table or card tables on a patio or on the lawn.

• Cover the tables with brightly colored plastic tablecloths.

• Mass fresh daisies, sunflowers, or zinnias in clear glass canning jars as the centerpiece.

• Have fun setting the tables. Use pie tins as dinner plates, pint-sized canning jars as glasses, and fingertip towels for napkins. In place of knives, forks, and spoons substitute various kitchen utensils, such as tongs, measuring spoons, a pie server, a spatula, an ice cream scoop, a wire whisk, etc.

• Large plastic "bibs" (like the ones used at seafood restaurants) are available at most restaurant supply businesses and will come in handy.

• Cover the set tables with large sheets until everyone is seated.

• As your guests arrive, take a picture of each

one, or each couple, to send to them later. A group portrait and a dinner shot will be most memorable.

• Seat your guests at the tables and remove the sheets covering the surprise place settings. Pass the food and let the fun begin.

• After dinner play this fun company game:

Ask each guest to put their name on a piece of paper and list three things about themselves that no one else knows.

As the host or hostess, read one of the items listed on someone's list (don't mention the name on the paper) and have the group guess who it is. Randomly go through the rest of the lists.

Read as many as time allows.

Tip: After your party, be ready for friendly retaliation.

Menu

Spaghetti with Ragu Bolognese Meat Sauce
Tossed Green Salad with
Cheesy Vinaigrette Salad Dressing
Fresh Fruit with Raspberry Fruit Dip
Tuscan Flat Bread
Lemon Sorbet

Ragu Bolognese Meat Sauce

INGREDIENTS

½ medium onion, diced

3 tablespoons olive oil

3 tablespoons butter

2 tablespoons diced celery

2 tablespoons diced carrot

2 mushrooms, diced

1 pound lean ground beef

½ cup milk

3 cans (8 ounces each) tomato sauce

pinch of oregano

pinch of dried parsley

salt to taste

In a deep, heavy, saucepan, sauté onions in the oil and butter just until soft. Add the celery, carrot, and mushrooms and cook gently for 2 minutes. Add the ground beef and crumble it in the pot with a fork. Cook just long enough for the meat to lose its raw, red color. Add the milk and cook on medium heat, stirring often, until the milk has evaporated. Add the tomato sauce and stir thoroughly. When the mixture begins to bubble, turn down the heat to low, or until the sauce cooks at the laziest simmer (just an occasional bubble). Cook, uncovered, for a minimum of 3½ to 4 hours, stirring occasionally. Towards the last of the simmering time, add the oregano and parsley. Taste and correct for salt.

Tip: Ragu can be kept in the refrigerator for up to 5 days, or frozen. Reheat until it simmers, for about 15 minutes.

Cheesy Vinaigrette Salad Dressing

INGREDIENTS

2 cups olive oil

11/4 cups red wine vinegar

1 pound blue cheese, crumbled

1 tablespoon garlic powder

1 tablespoon onion powder

2 teaspoons salt

2 teaspoons pepper

1 teaspoon parsley flakes

1 teaspoon oregano

Combine all ingredients in blender. Mix until smooth. Refrigerate.

Raspberry Fruit Dip

INGREDIENTS
1 container (8 ounces) frozen whipped topping, thawed
1 package (10 ounces) frozen raspberries, thawed

Gently fold raspberries and juice into the whipped topping. Serve immediately with fresh fruit.

Tip: Fresh fruit combinations of the same color add a different twist. For instance, combine honeydew melon, kiwi, Granny Smith apple slices, and green grapes; or cantaloupe, sliced peaches and nectarines, mango chunks, and papaya slices; or watermelon, raspberries, strawberries, and blueberries.

Tuscan Flat Bread

INGREDIENTS

1 tablespoon yeast

1 tablespoon sugar

2 cups warm water

4 cups flour

2 teaspoons salt

2 teaspoons crushed rosemary

½ cup melted butter

Preheat oven to 400 degrees. Dissolve yeast and sugar in warm water. Let sit for 2 to 3 minutes. Add flour, salt, and rosemary. Spread dough to the edges of a greased, lipped, jellyroll pan. Pour butter on dough and spread to cover all the dough. Let rise for 30 minutes. Bake for 20 minutes. Serve warm.

Tip: The rosemary could be omitted and the bread topped with Parmesan cheese before baking.

Lemon Sorbet

1²/₃ cups sugar
1½ cups water
1 tablespoon grated lemon peel
1 cup fresh lemon juice

Mix sugar, water, and lemon peel in heavy medium saucepan. Bring to a boil, stirring to dissolve sugar. Remove from heat. Stir in lemon juice; chill 1 hour. Process mixture in an ice cream maker according to manufacture instructions.

The first time I read an excellent book. it is to me Just
as if I had gained a new friend.

-Oliver Goldsmith

Children's Book Club

Having been a members of book clubs, we know the sheer pleasure of the whole process; reading the books, coming together as friends to review and discuss the books, and, of course, the visiting and refreshments. Why not create a venue for our children and grandchildren to learn to love books and reading? Start a book club especially for them. Begin now and gather interested participants. Then, once a month take turns hosting a Children's Book Club.

IDEAS

• Preschoolers and beginning readers up through third grade are fun to inspire and eager to learn, so start there.

• Children's books are usually short enough to read aloud during the club time.

• Invite adults to come to help keep order and to assist with the refreshments.

• Keep your group small, about 8 to 10 children, so there's enough room for everyone to be comfortable. Have all the children sit together on a large rug or a carpeted area.

• As the host or hostess of the book club, read the chosen book using your best funny voice or accent. Local libraries and bookstores are brimming with great books and help by suggesting titles.

• As you get going, your book club may want to try a few variations:

Pick numerous books centered on a single theme, author or character. One club meeting could be devoted to ballerinas, for example, or outer space. Next time, focus on the works of Dr. Seuss.

Have each child dress up as one of the characters you're reading about or according to the theme you're discussing. Let them dress as their all-time favorite book character and take turns sharing what they like about that character (mom or dad can dress up too). Talking about what they love about a character might inspire others to try a new book.

Ask everyone to bring a favorite book and choose someone to swap with. Before swapping, each child could explain why she picked that book. At the next meeting, compare notes and share thoughts about the swapped books.

Designate certain meetings as "Daddies Only" or "Grandparents Only". Kids can bring the special book that they share with that adult.

• Adjustments can certainly be made to make this idea work for older children.

Menu

PB&J Ribbon Sandwiches
Fresh Veggies with Dill Dip
Grandma Maud's Sugar Cookies
Or No Roll Sugar Cookies
Or Speedy Ice Cream Sandwiches
Berry Patch Punch

PB&J Ribbon Sandwiches

INGREDIENTS
3 loaves sandwich bread, cut horizontally into thirds
(order 1 pink, 1 light green, and 1 yellow from bakery)
Creamy peanut butter
Butter, softened
Favorite jam or jelly

Trim crusts from each loaf of bread. Assemble each ribbon loaf by placing a green layer of bread on a cutting board. Spread with peanut butter. Place a yellow layer of bread on top and spread lightly with butter and then jam or jelly. Spread a pink layer lightly with butter, and place buttered side on top of jam layer. Wrap loaf in plastic wrap and refrigerate.

To serve, cut loaves into 1-inch slices; cut each slice crosswise into halves.

Yield: 3 ribbon loaves.

Dill Dip

I N G R E D I E N T S

2 cups sour cream
1 cup salad dressing or mayonnaise
1 tablespoon parsley flakes
2 tablespoons dill weed
2 teaspoons minced onion

Blend all ingredients together until smooth. Chill. Serve with fresh vegetables.
Yield: 3 cups.

Grandma Maud's Sugar Cookies

INGREDIENTS

1 cup whipping cream
1 teaspoon vinegar
1 cup butter, softened
1 cup sugar
1 egg
1 teaspoon vanilla
1 teaspoon baking soda
1 teaspoon nutmeg (optional)
4 cups flour

Combine cream and vinegar in a small bowl and set aside. Cream together butter, sugar, egg, and vanilla. Add whipping cream mixed with soda and nutmeg. Mix well. Slowly add the flour. Roll dough out, cut into shapes, and place on ungreased cookie sheet. Bake at 400 degrees for 5 to 7 minutes until lightly browned on bottom only (the top shouldn't be browned). Frost and decorate with sprinkles or colored sugar.

Tip: For a unique look, cut dough using 4-inch and 2½-inch flower shaped cookie cutters, and a small 1¾-inch heart or circle cutter. These are approximate sizes. As soon as the cookies are baked, frosted and decorated, quickly assemble cookies as follows: place a 2½-inch cookie on top of a 4-inch cookie and a 1¾-inch cookie on top of the 2½-inch cookie, creating a layered look. A dab of frosting may be needed to adhere the cookies together. Allow cookies to stand 1 to 2 hours to set before serving. Store cookies unfrosted.

No Roll Sugar Cookies

INGREDIENTS
1 cup sugar
1 cup butter, softened
1 egg
1 teaspoon vanilla
2 cups flour
½ teaspoon baking soda
½ teaspoon cream of tartar
½ teaspoon salt
Sugar

Cream together 1 cup sugar, butter, egg, and vanilla. Add dry ingredients, and mix well. Batter will be sticky. Roll into balls the size of a walnut, and place on ungreased cookie sheet. Dip the bottom of a glass in sugar and press cookies to flatten slightly. Bake at 400 degrees for 8 to 10 minutes. Frost and decorate, if desired.

Yield: 3 dozen cookies.

Speedy Ice Cream Sandwiches

I N G R E D I E N T S

½ cup chopped malted milk balls

1 pint strawberry or vanilla ice cream, softened

12 soft cookies, such as chocolate, oatmeal or chocolate chip

(homemade or purchased)

6 tablespoons fudge ice cream topping

Stir chopped malted milk balls into the ice cream. Spoon ice cream on the flat side of six of the cookies. Spread 1 tablespoon of the fudge topping on the flat side of the other six cookies. Place cookie, fudge side down, onto ice cream. Wrap and freeze at least 6 hours, until firm. Let frozen sandwiches stand about 10 minutes before serving.

Yield: 6 servings.

Berry Patch Punch

INGREDIENTS
1 package berry flavored powdered drink mix

1 cup sugar

6 cups water

2 cans (12 ounces each) pink lemonade concentrate, thawed

2 cups pineapple juice

4 cans (12 ounces each) ginger ale, chilled

Dissolve powdered drink and sugar in water. Add lemonade concentrate and pineapple juice. Store in refrigerator. Just before serving, add ginger ale. Serve over ice.

Yield: 16 servings.

CELEBRATE FAMILY

September

Life affords no greater responsibility, no greater privilege, than the raising of the next generation.

—C. Everett Koop

Mothers & Daughters Afternoon Tea

Step back in time and enjoy a Mothers and Daughters Afternoon Tea. It can be a reason to wear a hat and dress up, after all, a tea is genteel—it's white lace, flowers, and mannerly behavior. You don't need to be bound by rules about what to serve. It is an opportunity to enjoy the company of daughters and special friends, some delightful food, and a chance to have a wonderful time.

IDEAS

• Search for a variety of cups and saucers, cream and sugar sets, plate holders, cake stands, and silver trays for displaying the sweets and sandwiches. Flea markets, antique stores, and garage sales are great places to find antique pieces. Search your cupboards and trunks for treasures to use, and, by all means, use what you already have, or borrow from a friend or relative. These accessories do most of the decorating for you. Just set the tables with simple linens—white if you have them—and use small arrangements of fresh flowers in silver julep cups or teapots. You can also use topiaries as centerpieces.

• Make unique favors using the teacups you've collected. "Plant" the cup by placing small squares of wheat grass (available in small planted flats at health food stores) in each cup. This should be done the morning of the party. Gently nest a chocolate in the grass. Place the cups on the tables at each seat, and slip a linen or paper napkin through the cup handle.

• Use clear, plain, or pastel glasses and plates if you have them.

• If you only have 8 to 10 people coming, set up a couple of tables and place a cake stand or a plate holder, and a silver tray or two, on each table. If more people are coming set up a buffet table with all the serving pieces. In the late afternoon a porch, patio, or lawn area would be a perfect setting.

• Use dainty ice cream dishes or frosted glasses to hold jams and clotted creams.

• Invite your guests to wear dresses and hats if desired.

• Use crystallized flowers or leaves for garnishes on the serving plates. Crystallized flowers and leaves can make wonderful decorations for cakes, desserts, and summer drinks. Pick leaves or flowers on a sunny, dry day. Remove stalks and the white bases from petals. Lightly beat an egg white until it starts to foam. Dip each flower or leaf into the egg white to coat (you may have to paint some of the flowers), then dip it into a dish of sugar. Once coated, place on a sheet of waxed paper on a wire cooling rack. Cover with another sheet of paper and place in a very low oven with the door left ajar. Store in an airtight tin when dry.

Flowers to crystallize:
Borage, cowslips, lavender, lilac, pansies, pinks, primroses, rose petals, rosemary, sage, violets.
Leaves to crystallize:
Bergamot, lemon balm, lemon verbena, mint.

Menu

Assorted Tea Sandwiches
Purchased Scones with Mock Clotted Cream or Lemon Curd
Or Crumpets with Butter Curls and Freezer Strawberry Jam
(page 53)
Toffee Pecan Bars
Brownie Tarts
Wonderful Little Walnut Cakes
Chocolate Crinkle Cups
Caramel Acorn Cookies
Lemon Savannah Cookies
Pretty in Pink Lemonade
French Hot Chocolate

Tea Sandwiches

I N G R E D I E N T S

Classic fillings include:

Sliced cucumber and cream cheese

Whipped cream cheese topped with smoked salmon and dill

Shredded chicken, minced carrots, and golden raisins mixed with
mayonnaise (serve as a small traditional sandwich)

Whipped cream cheese topped with crisp, crumbled bacon and a
lettuce leaf (serve as a small traditional sandwich)

Apricot preserves with minced ham

Bay shrimp and minced celery mixed with mayonnaise

Smoked turkey and avocado

Classic tea sandwiches are delicate, and almost bite-size. Start with very thinly sliced bread; frozen an hour or two before handling. Try different kinds of breads like raisin, egg, wheat, white, or mini corn muffins or rolls. Keep filling at room temperature for easier spreading. Spread bread first all the way out to the edges, then trim with a serrated knife and discard crusts. Cut bread into squares or triangles, or cut before filling into heart shapes, rounds, or flower shapes. Serve some open face and others as traditional sandwiches. The sandwiches should be made as close to serving time as possible to avoid sogginess. All of the filling ingredients should be thinly sliced or finely chopped for these dainty morsels.

Mock Clotted Cream

4 ounces whipped cream cheese
½ cup *un*salted butter, softened

Beat together cream cheese and butter in small bowl until well mixed. Cover and refrigerate until serving time.

Tip: Serve with English scones or crumpets.

Lemon Curd

3 eggs
¾ cup sugar
1 tablespoon grated lemon zest
1 cup fresh lemon juice
4 tablespoons cold butter, cut into 4 pieces

In a bowl or the top of a double boiler, whisk eggs until smooth. Whisk in sugar, zest, and lemon juice. Place over a small pan of simmering water; cook over low heat, stirring constantly with a wooden spoon until thick and pale yellow, about 7 to 10 minutes. Stir in butter, one tablespoon at a time until thoroughly combined and smooth. Remove from heat and set bowl over ice, stirring occasionally to cool. Cover with plastic wrap touching the surface and store in refrigerator up to 5 days.
Yield: 1½ cups.

Toffee Pecan Bars

INGREDIENTS
2 cups flour
½ cup powdered sugar
1 cup cold butter
1 egg
1 can sweetened condensed milk
1 teaspoon vanilla
1 package (8 ounces) English toffee pieces
1 cup coarsely chopped pecans

Preheat oven to 350 degrees. Combine flour and powdered sugar; cut in cold butter until mixture is crumbly. Press into a 9x13-inch pan. Bake for 15 minutes. Meanwhile, beat egg; add milk, vanilla, English toffee pieces, and pecans. Spread over baked crust; bake for another 20 minutes.

Yield: 24 bars.

Brownie Tarts

1 package chocolate fudge cake mix
½ cup butter, melted
1 egg
Filling (recipe on next page)

Preheat oven to 325 degrees. Spray mini muffin pans with cooking spray. Combine all ingredients and mix well. Scoop batter into muffin cups until two-thirds full. Bake 10 to 12 minutes, or until edges are set. Remove pan and press tops of brownies with a tart shaper (the plastic lid of a soda pop bottle works well), to make indentations. Cool in pan 15 minutes. Gently remove from pan. Cool. Cups will be firm. Pipe or spoon filling into formed cups. Store tightly covered in the refrigerator.

Yield: 36 tarts.

Tip: Best served when chilled. To serve, place a slice of fresh strawberry or a raspberry on top of each tart. Or, decorate tarts with chocolate sprinkles.

Brownie Tart Filling

1 small package instant chocolate pudding
1 cup half and half
1 container (8 ounces) frozen whipped topping, thawed

Mix pudding with half and half. Fold in whipped topping.

Wonderful Little Walnut Cakes

INGREDIENTS
1½ cups whipping cream, stiffly whipped
4 eggs, well beaten
1 cup ground walnuts
1 cake mix (yellow or white)
1 jar (12 ounces) raspberry preserves
Frosting (recipe on next page)

Fold cream into eggs. Stir walnuts into cake mix. Fold dry ingredients into egg and whipped cream mixture one-third at a time. Fill greased muffin pans half full (do not use paper liners). Bake 12 to 16 minutes at 350 degrees. To serve, invert and cut each cake in half horizontally to create two layers. Spread one teaspoon preserves between the two layers. Top with a tablespoon of frosting, allowing some to run down the sides. Garnish with a fresh berry and mint leaf, or a dime-sized dollop of preserves.

Walnut Cake Frosting

1½ cups whipping cream, stiffly whipped
1 package (8 ounces) cream cheese, softened
2 cups powdered sugar
⅛ teaspoon salt
1 teaspoon vanilla

Combine cream cheese, sugar, salt, and vanilla. Fold into whipped cream.

Chocolate Crinkle Cups

INGREDIENTS

1 package (6 ounces) semi-sweet chocolate chips
9 to 10 paper baking cups
Vegetable spray

Heat chocolate chips on low until partially melted. Remove from heat and stir until the chocolate is entirely melted. (Mixture should be thick, but if too thick return to heat for a few minutes.) Spray baking cups with vegetable spray. With a teaspoon, swirl the chocolate around the inside of the paper baking cups, covering the entire surface. Place cups in muffin pans and chill until firm. About ten minutes before serving, peel paper off the cups and fill with ice cream, pudding, or fruit.

Yield: 9 to 10 cups.

Caramel Acorn Cookies

INGREDIENTS

2¾ cups flour
½ teaspoon baking powder
1 cup butter, softened
¾ cup brown sugar, packed
3 egg yolks
1 teaspoon vanilla extract
½ cup finely chopped walnuts or pecans
½ pound caramels
¾ cup finely chopped walnuts or pecans

Preheat oven to 350 degrees. Mix together flour and baking powder. In medium mixing bowl, combine butter, brown sugar, and egg yolks. With an electric mixer, at medium speed, beat until smooth and fluffy. Using a wooden spoon, stir in vanilla, ½ cup nuts, and flour mixture. Mix well. For each cookie, shape one slightly rounded teaspoon of dough into a ball. With fingers, pinch dough to a rounded point at one end to resemble an acorn. Place one inch apart on ungreased baking sheet, pointed side up. Bake 15 to 18 minutes, or until golden brown. Remove from baking sheet to rack; cool completely. Combine caramels and ¼ cup water and microwave at one minute intervals until caramels are melted and mixture is smooth. Dip large end of cooled cookies into caramel, then into the ¾ cup nuts. Store covered in refrigerator. Yield: 75 cookies.

Lemon Savannah Cookies

INGREDIENTS
2 cups flour

¾ teaspoon baking soda

¼ teaspoon salt

¾ cup shortening or butter

1 cup sugar

2 package (3 to 4 ounces each) lemon instant pudding mix

3 eggs, slightly beaten

Preheat oven to 375 degrees. Combine flour, baking soda, and salt; set aside. Cream shortening and sugar; add pudding and beat until mixture is light and fluffy. Add eggs and mix thoroughly. Add dry ingredients and beat until well blended. Drop by teaspoonfuls onto a greased baking sheet about two and a half inches apart. Bake 8 minutes for a soft chewy cookie, and 10 minutes for a crispier cookie.

Yield: 6 dozen.

Pretty In Pink Lemonade

INGREDIENTS
Juice of 6 large lemons (1½ cups juice)
Juice of 2 limes (1/3 cup juice)
1¼ cups sugar
6 cups water
1 cup fresh raspberries
Lemon and Lime slices for garnish, optional

In a 2 quart pitcher, combine the lemon juice, lime juice, sugar, and water. Stir to dissolve. Add raspberries; cover and chill overnight. (The longer it sets, the pinker it is.) Serve over ice. Garnish with lemon and lime slices if desired.

Yield: 8 to 9 servings.

Tip: For fun, dip beverage glasses in lemon juice and then in pink colored sugar and let sit until firm.

French Hot Chocolate

½ cup semi-sweet chocolate pieces
½ cup light corn syrup
¼ cup water
1 teaspoon vanilla extract
1 pint whipping cream
2 quarts milk

In a saucepan, combine chocolate pieces, syrup, and water. Stir over low heat until chocolate pieces are melted. Pour chocolate mixture into a bowl and cool. Add vanilla extract. Whip cream, while gradually adding the chocolate mixture. Continue beating until mixture just mounds. Spoon fluffy chocolate whipped cream into a serving bowl and refrigerate. Just before serving, scald the milk and pour into a serving pitcher. To serve, spoon heaping tablespoons of chocolate mixture into each cup. Fill with hot milk and stir.

Did you know . . .
The custom of spooning the chocolate mixture into the cups first, before the hot liquid, grew out of the need to prevent fragile porcelain tea cups from cracking.

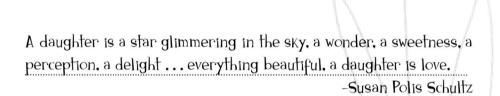

A daughter is a star glimmering in the sky, a wonder, a sweetness, a perception, a delight ... everything beautiful, a daughter is love.

-Susan Polis Schultz

Making Tracks–Fathers & Sons Outing

There aren't too many things that evoke childhood memories more than being out in nature; trampling leaves, rowing on a lake, going on a hike, finding wondrous treasures, or just listening to the utter stillness broken only by a bird's song. How quickly, amid the miracle of nature, we can remember and become children once again. Ensure that the children around you will have these memories too.

IDEAS

• Plan a trek out to the nearby woods, lake, or mountains. This is an enjoyable activity for relatives or a group of friends, or a special one-on-one time.

• Send an adult out just before the party and make "tracks" in the dirt or use "tracks" made from construction paper. At the end of the trail, leave a "treasure" to be found.

• En route, give the crew a list of things to search for as they are following the tracks. A few of these things may need to be "planted" beforehand. Take a bag along to carry these items back to base camp:

• Pine cone
• Acorns
• Leaves from a variety of trees
   ie: maple, oak, or apple
• A clump of moss
• A dried flower
• Nuts in the shell
• A rock shaped like something
• Metal tab from a soda can
• Rubber band
• Penny
• A frog
• Something shiny
• A piece of string
• Berries

• If your outing is close to any authorized fire pits, cook dinner while you're out. If not, a fire in a foil-lined wheelbarrow works great for a cookout.

• Remember to take pictures!

Menu

Roasted Hot Dogs

Chips

Vegetable Sticks

Joe Froggers (for the hike)

Apple Pie on a Stick

Swamp Water

Joe Froggers

INGREDIENTS

2¼ cups flour

1 teaspoon soda

½ teaspoon salt

1 teaspoon cinnamon

½ teaspoon ginger

½ cup shortening

¾ cup sugar

2 eggs

⅔ cup molasses

½ cup milk

Frosting (recipe on next page)

The name of the cookie comes from the South because the molasses cookies, when baked, humped up like a frog. Preheat oven to 375 degrees. Sift the flour, soda, salt, and spices together. Cream the shortening in a bowl. Add the sugar and cream until light and well blended. Add the eggs and beat well, then stir in the molasses. Add the flour mixture alternately with milk, mixing well after each addition. Drop by heaping teaspoonfuls onto greased baking sheet about two inches apart. Bake for 10 to 12 minutes. Cool.

Frogger Frosting

INGREDIENTS

½ cup butter or margarine

⅛ teaspoon salt

½ teaspoon ginger

3 cups powdered sugar

¼ cup molasses

2 tablespoons milk

Cream the butter in a bowl. Add the salt, ginger, and half of the sugar gradually, blending well after each addition. Add remaining sugar alternately with molasses and milk, beating after each addition until smooth. Add more milk if necessary. Beat until right consistency to spread. Frost top of each cookie.

Apple Pie On A Stick

INGREDIENTS

1 cup sugar
1 tablespoon cinnamon
Several Apples
Roasting Sticks

Mix sugar and cinnamon; set aside. Push the stick or dowel through the top of the apple until the apple is secure on the stick. Place the apple two to three inches above the hot coals and turn the apple while roasting it. As the apple cooks, the skin starts to brown and the juice comes out. When the skin in loose, remove the apple from the fire but leave it on the stick. Peel the skin off the apple, being careful not to burn yourself. Roll the apple in the sugar and cinnamon mixture, then return it to roast over the coals, letting the sugar and cinnamon form a glaze over the apple. Remove the apple from the coals and let it cool. Slice off pieces and eat.

Swamp Water

INGREDIENTS
Green punch, limeade, or lemonade.

Serve it in small canning jars or tin cups.

CELEBRATE FRIENDS
October

Double, double toil and trouble; fire burn and cauldron bubble. —Shakespeare

Witches Night Out

When you see a witch passing in front of the moon, she isn't riding just any broom. A witch's broom is called a Besom. It has a tree limb for a broomstick, twigs for bristles, and flexible branches securing the twigs to the handle. Invite your very nicest "witch" friends or family to fly their besoms over to celebrate your friendship with a whimsical Halloween party.

IDEAS

• Pumpkin possibilities:

Spray paint a pumpkin with 14-carat gold spray paint, available at craft stores. Cover the entire surface, or merely dust the tops of the pumpkins. Leave plain, or decorate around the stem with flowers or a festive ribbon.

Paint small pumpkins with white glue and roll in ultra fine glitter until the entire surface is coated.

• A few weeks before the party, invite your friends or family and ask them to think of a service they would be willing to auction off at the party. For instance: babysitting, computer help, etc. Have everyone fill out a Certificate of Service paper stating the service that they will offer for the auction. Conduct the service auction. Give everyone 15 beans to use for bidding.

• Make favors beforehand:

Trinket balls: Secure one end of a roll of Halloween colored paper to a 3 or 4-inch Styrofoam ball with a straight pin or tape. Wind the paper tightly around the ball and tuck trinkets (available at novelty and craft stores) in between the paper as you round the ball several times. Then, snip the crepe paper and secure with tape. Tie a contrasting ribbon around the ball.

Goodie cones: Cut 10-inch squares of Halloween colored card stock. Wind each square into a cone and staple. Cut across the top to even out the opening. Punch out two holes on the cone top to thread a ribbon handle through. Fill with goodies.

• Create a floral centerpiece by slicing off the top several inches of a pumpkin, saving the lid. Remove the seeds and pulp and rinse interior. Fill the pumpkin with water and arrange with flowers. Set the pumpkin on a bed of moss. For a dazzling effect, make several pumpkin "vases" and fill each one with a different variety of flowers.

• For another centerpiece idea, push the bottom ends of several medium sized swirled Halloween lollipops into the top area of a pumpkin.

• A buffet works best for this dinner. Prepare the soups in cauldrons and the guests can choose which one they would like.

• As an activity, have everyone decorate a small sized pumpkin you have already sprayed gold.

• As your guests leave, present them with a package of homemade Black Licorice Caramels (recipe follows). Use your creativity in decorating the packages.

Menu

Italian Sausage Soup
Creamy Chicken Noodle Soup
Clam Chowder
Orange and Kiwi Salad
Broomsticks
Caramel Baked Apples
Crunchy Caramel Corn
Black Licorice Caramels
Citrus Cooler

Italian Sausage Soup

2 boxes (32 ounces each) chicken broth
2 cups julienne carrots
2 cups frozen French style green beans
1 package (9 ounces) three cheese tortellini
1 pound pork sausage, browned and drained
1 tablespoon Italian seasoning
Pesto Sauce for garnish, optional

Combine all ingredients except pesto sauce in a large pot; bring to a boil and cook for 15 minutes. Add more water if necessary. Top with pesto, if desired.

Yield: 6 servings.

Creamy Chicken Noodle Soup

2½ quarts water

6 chicken flavor bouillon cubes or 2 tablespoons chicken flavor instant bouillon

6½ cups uncooked egg noodles

2 cans (10¾ ounces each) cream of chicken soup

3 to 4 chicken breasts, cooked and diced

1 container (8 ounces) sour cream

Parsley flakes for garnish

In a large saucepan, combine the water and the bouillon cubes; bring to a boil. Add the noodles and cook uncovered for 10 minutes, or until noodles are tender. Add soup and chicken; heat thoroughly. Add more bouillon, if necessary, to taste. Remove from heat; add sour cream and stir to blend. Sprinkle with parsley just before serving.

Yield: 6 to 8 servings.

Clam Chowder

INGREDIENTS

2 cans (8 ounces each) minced clams
2 cups diced potatoes
1 cup chopped onion
1 cup diced celery
¾ cup butter
¾ cup flour
1 pint whipping cream or 2 pints half and half
1 pint milk
1½ teaspoons salt
½ teaspoon sugar
Pepper to taste

Drain liquid from clams and pour over vegetables. Add water to barely cover; cook until tender. Melt butter; add flour, and blend well. Stir in cream and milk; cook, stirring constantly, until smooth and thick. Add vegetables and clams (without draining); heat thoroughly. Season with salt, sugar, and pepper. Add more milk if soup becomes too thick.
Yield: 6 servings.

Orange And Kiwi Salad

INGREDIENTS

1 head romaine lettuce, torn into bite-size pieces (6 cups)
2 kiwi fruit, peeled and cut into slices
2 oranges, peeled and cut into sections
½ medium red onion, sliced
Poppy Seed Dressing (recipe on next page)

In large bowl, toss dressing with the salad ingredients. Serve immediately.

Yield: 6 Servings.

Tip: In the winter, when pomegranates are in season, ¼ cup pomegranate seeds look festive scattered on top of the salad.

Tip: Make the dressing; cover and refrigerate. Up to 6 hours ahead, put the greens, fruit and onion in the serving bowl; cover with a damp paper towel and plastic wrap and refrigerate. Just before serving, shake the dressing well and toss it with the salad.

Poppy Seed Dressing

INGREDIENTS

½ cup mayonnaise

⅓ cup sugar

¼ cup milk

2 tablespoons white vinegar

1 tablespoon poppy seeds

In a small bowl, combine all ingredients and beat with a wire whisk. Refrigerate dressing.

Broomsticks

INGREDIENTS

12 (¼-inch diameter) dowels, 18 in. long (washed and dried)

24 frozen dinner rolls, thawed but still cold (thaw in refrigerator)

½ cup butter, melted

½ teaspoon garlic salt

½ teaspoon dill

Combine butter, garlic salt, and dill in a bowl and let stand to mingle flavors. Press two rolls together and roll into a rope 12 to 14 inches long. Beginning at one end of the dowel, wrap one end of the dough over the end to secure the dough to the dowel. Twist the dough down the dowel about three-quarters the length of the dowel. Place "broomsticks" on a greased cookie sheet and let rise 30 minutes. Bake at 350 degrees for 12 to 15 minutes, or until lightly browned. Remove from oven and generously brush the hot rolls on both sides with the garlic-dill butter. Remove the "broomsticks" from the pan and stand them up in three or four tall sturdy glasses, mugs, or vases. Serve warm.

Yield: 12

Caramel Baked Apples

INGREDIENTS
1 package (14 ounces) caramels (49 to 50 caramels)
1/3 cup heavy whipping cream
1 tablespoon butter
6 to 8 medium baking apples

In a glass bowl, combine caramels and cream. Microwave on high for 3 minutes. Stir until smooth and fully melted, add butter and stir to combine. Preheat oven to 350 degrees (325 degrees if using a glass pan). Peel and core the apples. Slice the top and bottom of each apple so that it can stand flat on either end. Arrange the apples in a roasting pan, deep baking dish, or casserole dish. Pour the caramel sauce all over the apples and seal the dish with foil or a tight fitting lid. Bake for 20 minutes. Remove apples from oven and turn each one over using tongs. Spoon sauce over each apple, re-seal the pan and bake for another 20 minutes. Test for doneness by piercing with the point of a paring knife. The apples should be tender all the way through, but not mushy. If necessary, bake for another few minutes. To serve, stand each apple upright in individual dishes, pour remaining caramel sauce over the apples and top with a scoop of vanilla ice cream, if desired.

Yield: 6 to 8 servings.

Tip: The apples can be baked a day in advance and refrigerated. Reheat the apples and sauce in a 350 degree oven for 8 to 10 minutes or in a microwave oven for 2 to 5 minutes.

Crunchy Caramel Corn

1½ cups butter
1½ cups brown sugar
½ cup light corn syrup
½ teaspoon salt
½ teaspoon soda
6 quarts popcorn

Combine butter, brown sugar, corn syrup and salt in a large heavy pan. Bring to a boil over medium heat and boil, stirring constantly, for five minutes. Remove from heat and add soda, mixing well. Pour caramel mixture over popcorn a little at a time and stir to coat well. Transfer caramel corn into a large rectangular pan. Bake for 1 hour at 250 degrees, stirring every 15 minutes. Spread popcorn onto waxed paper and separate kernels; cool completely. Store in a airtight container or plastic bags. Will stay fresh for several days.

Yield: 6 quarts caramel corn

Black Licorice Caramels

INGREDIENTS

1 can sweetened condensed milk

2 cups sugar

1 cup butter

¼ teaspoon salt

1½ cups light corn syrup

½ teaspoon black paste food coloring

½ teaspoon (generous) anise oil

Combine the first 5 ingredients in a heavy pan. Cook, stirring constantly over medium heat, until the mixture reaches 230 degrees on a candy thermometer. Take pan off the heat and add the black paste food color and anise oil. Pour into a buttered 9x13-inch pan. When cool, cut into small pieces and wrap in wax paper.

Tip: The black food paste coloring and anise oil can be found at candy making supply stores. They work much better than regular food coloring and licorice flavoring. You can also purchase precut papers to wrap the caramels in at the same store.

Citrus Cooler

INGREDIENTS

1 quart water

3 cups sugar

1 tablespoon citric acid (found in the pharmacy)

1 tablespoon pure lemon extract

Combine all ingredients and mix until sugar is dissolved. Pour into a punch bowl with lots of ice or over ice in individual glasses.

Yield: 20 glasses (8 ounces each)

Tip: Float orange, lemon, or lime slices; or raspberries and mint sprigs; or rinsed pansies, rose petals, or nasturtiums in the punch bowl.

Share a Treasure Brunch

A brunch offers friends time to visit and catch up before school gets out and the day's busy activities loom before them. The term "brunch" was introduced in 1895 in a British magazine called *Hunter's Weekly*. It was defined as a combination of breakfast and lunch, and was eaten after a hunt. The dishes served at a brunch can vary from traditional breakfast fare to more substantial lunch cuisine, or a combination of both.

IDEAS

• When you invite your friends over, ask each one to bring something that means a lot to them, like an heirloom, a special gift from a child or parent, or any item that they treasure. Explain that they will be sharing its importance to the group.

• When setting the table, use family heirlooms if you have them. Children's silver cups or teacups could be used to hold a flower by each person's place; a few one of a kind dishes could be utilized as serving pieces; and demitasse spoons could be used for jam. If you have full place settings of silverware, china, or crystal, so much the better. Keep the look somewhat light and feminine.

• Try this creative centerpiece idea. Place jelly beans (colors to compliment your table décor), or other types of candy, between two glass nesting vases.

Fill the inside vase with water and mass cut flowers such as mums, asters, calla lilies, ornamental kale, or greenery. A small potted plant or flower can be slipped right into the vase.

• Tag the stems of miniature white pumpkins with your guests names on them; place them on the plates as place cards. Apples or pears would be good alternatives to the pumpkins.

- As the guests arrive, display the items they bring on a table nearby for all to admire. After the brunch, have them share the stories of their treasures.

- Send a "take home" treasure with each guest. Write the recipes you've used on note cards and tie them with a length of ribbon. Give them to guests as they leave.

Fall offers so many natural beauties to make decorating a snap:

- Pile large pumpkins in a wheelbarrow and place in the garden area or by the front porch.

- Plant pots of fall flowers or decorative kale or cabbage; tuck pie-pumpkins or sugar-pumpkins around the flowers and place a small tree branch toward the back of the pots. Showcase the pots by the front door.

- Nestle one or two miniature pumpkins in places all around the kitchen or living area. Line them up on windowsills, on mantles, or tables. Tuck them in indoor plants or snuggle together several in a basket.

Menu

Breakfast Casserole
Refrigerated Blueberry Muffins
Or Buttermilk Coffee Cake
Red and Green Grapes
Hot Cranberry Cider

Breakfast Casserole

1 package (30 ounces) frozen hash browns, thawed (shredded works best)
½ cup melted butter
1½ cups Monterey Jack cheese shredded
1½ cups cheddar cheese, shredded
1½ cups cubed Black Forest ham (2 thick slices)
6 eggs
1 cup evaporated milk or cream
½ teaspoon seasoned salt

In a greased 9x13-inch pan, layer potatoes. Pour melted butter over potatoes. Bake at 400 degrees for 25 minutes. Remove from oven and cool. Layer ham and cheeses over potatoes. Mix eggs, cream, and salt; pour on top. Bake at 350 degrees for 30 to 40 minutes. Cover with foil if eggs get too brown.

Yield: 12 servings.

Tip: Casserole can be refrigerated after the potatoes have cooked. Finish by baking the next day.

Refrigerated Blueberry Muffins

I N G R E D I E N T S

2/3 cup shortening

1 cup sugar

3 eggs

3 cups flour

3 heaping teaspoons baking powder

1 teaspoon salt

1 cup milk

1½ cups fresh or frozen blueberries

Cream the shortening and sugar until fluffy. Add the eggs, one at a time, beating well after each addition. Sift together the flour, baking powder, and salt. Add the dry ingredients alternately with milk. When well blended, fold in the blueberries. This mixture will keep in the refrigerator for 2 to 3 weeks. Bake in greased muffin tins at 375 degrees for 15 to 20 minutes. Yield: 4 dozen.

Buttermilk Coffee Cake

INGREDIENTS

½ cup pecan pieces

2 teaspoons cinnamon

1½ cups flour

⅓ cup sugar

½ cup brown sugar

½ teaspoon ground ginger

1 teaspoon cinnamon

7 tablespoons butter, softened

1 egg

⅔ cups buttermilk

½ teaspoon baking soda

½ teaspoon baking powder

½ teaspoon salt

Preheat oven to 350 degrees. In a small bowl, combine pecans and 2 teaspoons cinnamon. In another, combine flour, sugars, ginger, 1 teaspoon cinnamon, and salt; stir until thoroughly mixed. Cut butter in with a fork or pastry cutter. Remove ⅔ cup of this mixture from the bowl and add this to the pecans and cinnamon; stir and set aside. Beat egg into the large bowl of flour mixture, then gradually add the buttermilk. At this point, it is very important to whip the batter until it is light and smooth. Stir the baking soda and baking powder into the batter, stirring well. Pour the batter into a well greased and parchment paper lined 9-inch round cake pan spreading the batter evenly. Cover the top with the crumb mixture. Place the coffee cake in the oven and bake for 25 minutes, or until cake tester comes out clean. Do not disturb the cake while baking. Cool 5 minutes before removing from pan.

Yield: 10 to 12 servings.

Hot Cranberry Cider

I N G R E D I E N T S
Honey butter (recipe on next page)
2 bottles (about 48 ounces each) cranberry juice cocktail
1½ quarts apple juice or apple cider
2 large oranges, unpeeled, thinly sliced

Prepare honey butter mixture; set aside. Combine the cranberry juice and apple juice; heat, uncovered, over medium heat, stirring occasionally, until mixture just comes to a boil. For each serving, spoon 1 scant tablespoon of the honey butter into the bottom of a 6 ounce mug and fill with the hot cranberry mixture. Cut orange slices in half and float one half in each cup. For a single serving, spoon honey butter into a mug, add half of an orange slice, and fill with cold cranberry juice mixture. Heat in a microwave oven 1½ to 2 minutes until mixture is hot.

Yield: 4½ quarts.

Honey Butter

INGREDIENTS
¾ cup butter or margarine
¾ cup honey
4 tablespoons ground coriander

Combine butter or margarine, honey, and coriander in a small saucepan and cook over low heat, stirring often, until butter melts. Or microwave butter or margarine, honey, and coriander 1 to 1½ minutes on full power until butter melts; remove and stir to blend.

November

Memories remind us of the journeys we have taken and the people we have loved. —Unknown

Bring a Memory Get-Together

Usually, family members are the people we share the most memories with, and it's that very concept that makes this get-together so enjoyable. Plus, you are making still more memories. Invite the couples, or adult members of your family for a late Saturday afternoon and evening event. You'll want the extra time to visit and enjoy the activities.

IDEAS

• When you extend invitations to the party, ask each family member to bring copies of their favorite photographs from throughout the year like vacations, birthdays, family parties, weddings, graduations, and birth announcements. As you begin this tradition, you may also want your family to bring special photos and family memories of the past.

• Decorate the house with a warm, late fall look using embellishments of tree branches, berry and flower bouquets, and milk chocolate colored bows. Tie a clutch of colorful berries and greenery together with natural colored twine and hang on the front door.

• Keep up the pumpkin decorations suggested in the October chapter. They move nicely into November decorating ideas.

• For the table, start by centering two pillar candleholders, about 8 to 10 inches tall, on the table. Place deep yellow pillar candles on the holders, encircled by rings of fresh seeded eucalyptus leaves and pyracantha berries.

Between the candleholders, and on either end, place weathered clay or cement pots brimming with small tangerines and kumquats paired with a few branches of seeded eucalyptus. Mix olive green, golden yellow, and burnt orange ceramic plates and striped goblets in the same colors. Mosaic glass votives scattered around the table echo the autumn hues.

• Decorative cards and a pen placed by each plate invite guests to write down the things they are most thankful for this year. Let family members share their thoughts before dinner; afterward, place the cards in a special family scrapbook everyone will be compiling later.

• After the meal, set out a blank scrapbook along with supplies like pens, markers, adhesive, and fun scrapbooking accessories. Then, let each family member add their photographs to the book and write notes about the pictures. Also include the cards that your guests filled out before dinner.

• As you assemble the scrapbook, you'll be enjoying each others pictures and memories, and deepening your relationships. Send the book home with the grandparents to look at and treasure. Then each year as the scrapbook is brought back to your family get-together and shared once again, you will have an on-going history of your family.

• Each year the family gathering can rotate to another's home.

• One year everyone can bring a favorite food that has a special memory attached with it.

Menu

Pot Roast with Vegetables
Green Beans Supreme
Crimson Crunch Salad
Golden Pumpkin Rolls
Lemon Lush
Or Melted Ice Cream Mousse

Pot Roast With Vegetables

INGREDIENTS
1 Tri-tip roast (about ½ pound per person)
2 tablespoons vegetable oil
1 large onion (or dried to equal)
3 to 5 cloves garlic, minced (or dried to equal)
Salt and Pepper, optional
2 bay leaves
3 to 4 potatoes, peeled and quartered
½ bag baby carrots
1 cup water
1 to 3 tablespoons instant beef bouillon granules

In a roasting pan, brown roast on both sides in oil. Salt and pepper a little if desired. Cover roast with onion and garlic; add bay leaves. Top with potatoes and carrots. Pour water over all. Cover and simmer on low for 4 to 5 hours. About 1 hour before serving, add enough hot water, with the bouillon dissolved in it, to make 3 cups of gravy. Before serving, remove the bay leaves, dish up the potatoes, carrots, and roast; strain liquid and make gravy (recipe on next page).

Pot Roast Gravy

2 tablespoons cornstarch
3 tablespoons cold water

Dissolve cornstarch in the cold water. Stir into liquid in pan and cook over medium heat until thickened.

Green Beans Supreme

INGREDIENTS

½ cup sliced onion

1 tablespoon minced parsley

2 tablespoons butter or margarine

2 tablespoons flour

2 teaspoons salt

¼ teaspoon pepper

½ tablespoon grated lemon peel

1 cup sour cream

5 cups green beans (canned or cooked), drained

½ cup grated cheese

2 tablespoons melted butter

½ cup dry bread crumbs

Cook onion and parsley in butter until tender. Add flour, salt, pepper, and lemon peel. Add sour cream and mix well. Add beans and heat. Spoon into baking dish. Top with grated cheese. Combine melted butter and bread crumbs; sprinkle over beans. Broil until cheese melts and crumbs brown.

Yield: 6 servings.

Crimson Crunch Salad

INGREDIENTS

1 package (6 ounces) cherry gelatin
1 can (16 ounces) whole cranberry sauce
1 can (20 ounces) crushed pineapple, drained, reserve juice
3 apples, peeled and diced
2 pomegranates, seeded, reserving 1/3 cup seeds for garnish
Or 1 cup chopped pecans (optional)
1 package (8 ounces) cream cheese, softened
1/3 cup sugar
1 container (12 ounces) frozen whipped topping, thawed

Make gelatin according to instructions on the package, substituting the reserved pineapple juice for the cold water. Add cranberry sauce, pineapple, apples, and pomegranate seeds or nuts. Place in an oblong pan; chill until set. Whip cream cheese until light; add sugar and mix well. Fold in whipped topping. Spread over set gelatin salad; sprinkle remaining pomegranate seeds on the top.

Yield: 12 servings.

Tip: In order to remove the seeds from the pomegranate easily, cut off the blossom end, score the sides of the fruit, and submerge in cold water for a minute or two.

Golden Pumpkin Rolls

1 package active dry yeast
2 cups flour
1½ cups milk
2 tablespoons shortening
2 tablespoons sugar
1½ teaspoons salt
1 egg, slightly beaten
⅓ cup canned pumpkin (not pumpkin pie filling)
Melted butter

In a large mixer bowl combine, yeast and flour. In a saucepan heat the milk, shortening, sugar, and salt. Stir constantly until shortening is almost melted; cool to about 120 degrees. Add to dry mixture; then add egg and pumpkin. Beat at low speed with mixer for 30 seconds, scraping sides of bowl constantly. Beat at high speed for 3 minutes. Add more flour, if needed, to make a soft dough. Divide dough into thirds; roll each third into a 12-inch circle. Brush each with melted butter and cut into 12 pie shaped wedges. Roll up wedge starting with the wide end. Place point side down on greased baking sheets. Brush with melted butter. Cover, let rise until light, (about one hour). Bake in a preheated, 400 degree oven for 10 to 12 minutes. Yield: 36 rolls.

Lemon Lush

INGREDIENTS

½ cup butter or margarine
1 cup finely chopped nuts
1 cup flour
1 package (8 ounces) cream cheese
1 cup powdered sugar
2 containers (8 ounces each) frozen whipped topping, thawed
3 packages (3.4 ounces each) instant lemon pudding mix
3 cups cold milk

Preheat oven to 350 degrees. Combine butter or margarine, nuts, and flour; press into a 9x13-inch pan. Bake for 15 minutes; let cool. Beat cream cheese and powdered sugar; add 1 container whipped topping, and mix well. Spread over cooled crust. Stir together lemon pudding mix and milk; spread on top of cream cheese mixture. Spread the other container of whipped topping over the pudding. Refrigerate.

Yield: 16 to 20 servings.

Tip: This can be made well ahead of time. Cover and keep refrigerated.

Melted Ice Cream Mousse

INGREDIENTS

1 pint chocolate ice cream

1 cup whipping cream

1/3 cup unsweetened cocoa powder

Place ice cream in a medium saucepan. Heat over low heat until melted. Transfer to an extra large mixing bowl; cover and chill about 1 hour, or until cold. Add whipping cream to melted ice cream. Beat with an electric mixer on high speed for 5 to 6 minutes, or until soft peaks begin to form. (Don't give up; it will work.) Sift cocoa powder into the chocolate mixture. Beat on low speed for 2 minutes—scraping the sides of the bowl twice—until combined and stiff peaks form. Pour into serving bowl. Cover and chill 1 to 6 hours and serve.

Yield: 6 to 8 servings

May we take time to give thanks for the gift of this sweet life, and for the wisdom of those who have helped us to see it more clearly.

-Unknown

Memory Lane

Take a trip down memory lane with your grandparents, your children's grandparents, or both. Learn more about them and let them know how much you love and appreciate them. As an added bonus, the grandparents will have the chance to pass along a memory they have of you!

IDEAS

• A while before the party, have each child decorate a small shoebox to be used for a special surprise. Ask the grandparents to write a memory or two they have of each child, growing up last year or last week. The boxes will be used to hold written memories or pictures after the night of the dinner.

• Plan a surprise for Grandma and Grandpa, too. Videotape family members telling a favorite story about them. Show the tape the night of the party and present them with a copy. You and other family members might want a copy also.

• Decorate the house with pictures of your grandparents, some current and others when they were younger. Play music from their era, such as Big Band, Swing, Charleston, or Rock 'n' Roll.

• After dinner, videotape Grandma and Grandpa sharing stories of their youth, how they met each other, things they did together, etc. Make copies for everyone. Take lots of pictures too.

• Have Grandma and Grandpa read the memories they have written about each grandchild, and then give each child the stories to put in their special memory boxes.

Of all the moments we gather in our lives, the ones we cherish most are the moments shared.
—Unknown

Menu

Parmesan Chicken

Steak House Potatoes Au Gratin

Veggie Melts

Lacquered Citrus Salad

Fresh Cranberry Relish

Angel Pecan Pie

Or Southern Banana Puddin'

Parmesan Chicken

INGREDIENTS

6 skinless, boneless chicken breasts
4 tablespoons melted butter
1½ cups cornflake crumbs
Parmesan cheese

Dip chicken breasts in the butter and then roll in cornflake crumbs. Place in a foil lined, oblong pan. Sprinkle with Parmesan cheese. Bake at 350 degrees for 30 minutes.
Yield: 6 servings.

Steak House Potatoes Au Gratin

INGREDIENTS

1 cup whipping cream

½ cup milk

1½ tablespoons flour

1 large clove garlic, pressed

⅛ teaspoon salt

⅛ teaspoon pepper

1 tablespoon butter, softened

3 to 4 medium russet potatoes

1½ cups grated cheddar cheese

1 teaspoon chopped fresh parsley

Preheat oven to 400 degrees. In a bowl, combine the cream, milk, flour, garlic, and pepper; beat by hand until well mixed. Coat the inside of a large baking dish with the softened butter. Peel the potatoes and cut into ¼-inch slices; quarter each of those slices. Arrange one fourth of the potatoes on the bottom of the dish. Pour some of the cream mixture over the potatoes. Repeat this layering step three more times. Cover the potatoes and bake for 20 minutes. Uncover; bake another 40 minutes, or until potatoes are starting to brown on top. Sprinkle cheese over the top of the potatoes and continue baking for 5 to 10 minutes, or until cheese melts and potatoes are tender. Sprinkle with parsley; serve.

Yield: 6 to 8 servings.

Veggie Melts

1 cup sliced fresh broccoli

¾ cup shredded zucchini

1 cup shredded carrots

2 tablespoons chopped celery

1 cup cauliflower flowerets

2 tablespoons melted butter

1 cup shredded Monterey Jack cheese

1 cup shredded cheddar cheese

1 can (2.8 ounces) French fried onion rings

1 tablespoon bacon bits

Combine vegetables in bowl. Pour butter over vegetables and toss. Spoon into microwave safe dish. Microwave on high 4 minutes. Top with cheeses, onion rings, and bacon bits. Cover and microwave on high 1 to 2 minutes, or until cheese melts.

Yield: 6 to 8 servings.

Lacquered Citrus Salad

I N G R E D I E N T S

1½ cups sugar
1½ teaspoons lemon juice
½ cup water
¼ teaspoon ground cardamom
1 teaspoon vanilla extract
3 ruby red grapefruit
3 navel oranges
1 lime

Combine the sugar, lemon juice, water, and cardamom in a medium saucepan. Bring to a simmer and cook until the sugar is dissolved. Remove from heat and add the vanilla. Steep for 20 minutes. Cut the peel and white pith from the grapefruit and oranges. Section the fruit by cutting the fruit away from the membrane. Arrange the fruit on a serving platter. Finely grate the zest from the lime and sprinkle it on the fruit. Spoon about half of the syrup over the salad; serve additional syrup on the side.

Yield: 6 servings.

Tip: This sugary sauce is also wonderful over strawberries, raspberries, blueberries, and black-berries.

Fresh Cranberry Relish

INGREDIENTS

1 package cranberries, frozen for easier grinding

3 apples, peeled and cored

3 cups sugar

2 oranges, peeled and chopped

½ cup crushed pineapple, drained

1 package frozen strawberries, thawed and drained, reserve juice

1 package (3 ounces) raspberry gelatin, dissolved in reserved
strawberry juice

½ cup chopped pecans

Grind cranberries and apples and mix well. Add sugar and let juice about 2 to 3 hours. Add oranges, pineapple, strawberries, gelatin, and pecans, mixing well. Put in sterilized jars and refrigerate. Will keep in refrigerator 4 to 6 weeks. Can also be frozen.

Tip: Freeze extra jars to be used throughout the year. The relish would be tasty with the Stuffed Pork Chops featured in the February menu.

Angel Pecan Pie

INGREDIENTS

3 egg whites
1 cup granulated sugar
1/8 teaspoon salt
¾ cup soda cracker crumbs
1 teaspoon baking powder
¾ cup pecans
1 teaspoon vanilla
½ cup whipping cream, whipped and sweetened

Preheat oven to 350 degrees. Beat egg whites until very stiff; add sugar and salt. Beat again until stiff. Fold in soda cracker crumbs and baking powder. Fold in broken pecans and vanilla. Bake for exactly 35 minutes in an ungreased pie pan. When cool, frost with sweetened whipped cream. Let set at least 3½ hours—better if left overnight.

Yield: 6 servings.

Southern Banana Puddin'

INGREDIENTS
1 package (5.1 ounces) instant vanilla pudding
1 container (16 ounces) frozen whipped topping, thawed
1 box (12 ounces) vanilla wafers, broken into fourths
5 bananas, sliced

In a large bowl, mix pudding according to instructions on box; fold in whipped topping. Add vanilla wafers and bananas; gently combine. Refrigerate at least 4 hours, or overnight.
Yield: 10–12 servings.
Tip: This makes a large quantity, but can easily be cut in half.

December

For unto you is born this day in the city of David a Saviour, which is Christ the Lord. —Luke 2:11

Holy Christmas Supper

Christmas is a season for time-honored family traditions and heightened anticipation for little ones. To help slow the pace and ease the frenzy of excitement, celebrate Christmas Eve in a different way. Gather your family and share a meal that would have been served in Christ's time.

IDEAS

• Place luminaries (white paper sacks weighted with sand, and then a votive candle placed on top of sand) along the driveway and walkway to the front door.

• Set the table with brown linens or placemats.

• Use a wicker paper plate holder with a paper napkin placed on top as a plate. Place another napkin by the side of the wicker holder.

• Use stoneware mugs

• Eat with fingers, no silverware

• Dine by candlelight

• Discuss the true meaning of Christmas while eating

The food suggested is not totally authentic and seems sparse when compared to what we usually eat. However, in Christ's time it would have been considered a feast. Of course, substitutions can be made to meet the needs of your family.

FOOD AND MEANING:

Leg of lamb or fish
  The Savior
Horseradish (Bitter Herb)
  Bondage and slavery of Israel in Egypt
Sliced Boiled Eggs

Beginning of Life
Unleavened Bread (pita bread)
    Bread of life, The Savior
Challah or Cracker Bread
Honey, Cheese, Olives
    Commonly eaten at Christ's time
Grapes, Dates, and Figs
Baklava
    Commonly eaten at Christ's time
Grape Juice
    Blood of Christ shed for us

Menu

Leg of Lamb or fish
Horseradish
Sliced Boiled Eggs
Unleavened Bread
Challah or Cracker Bread
Grapes, Date, and Figs
Baklava
Grape Juice

Challah

INGREDIENTS

2 packages yeast
½ cup lukewarm water
6 tablespoons shortening
1½ cups scalded milk
2 tablespoons sugar
2 teaspoons salt
3 eggs
6½ to 7 cups flour
Poppy seeds (Optional)

Dissolve yeast in lukewarm water. Set aside. Melt shortening in scalded milk. Pour into a large mixing bowl. Add sugar and salt. Let cool to lukewarm. Mix eggs into yeast, reserving 1 yolk. Add egg and yeast mixture to milk mixture. Stir in 4 cups flour and mix well. Add remaining flour, half a cup at a time, until dough begins to leave sides of bowl. Turn onto floured board and knead dough until smooth and elastic, about 5 minutes. Place dough in well-greased bowl. Oil top of dough. Cover with a towel, and let rise until double in bulk, about 1½ hours. Punch down. Divide into three parts. Divide each third into three parts. Roll dough and braid into three loaves. Place each braided loaf in a pan. Mix reserved egg yolk with 1 tablespoon cold water. Brush over the loaves. Sprinkle with poppy seeds (optional). Set aside and let rise one hour. Bake at 375 degrees for 45 to 60 minutes, or until loaves sound hollow when tapped and are lightly browned.
Yield: 3 loaves.

Cracker Bread

5½ to 6 cups flour, divided

1 package dry yeast

1 tablespoon sugar

1½ teaspoons salt

2 cups warm water (105 to 115 degrees)

⅓ cup butter, melted

2 tablespoons sesame seeds, toasted

Combine 4 cups flour, yeast, sugar, and salt in a large mixing bowl; stir well. Gradually add water to flour mixture. Add butter; beat. Gradually stir in enough remaining flour to make a stiff dough. Turn dough out on a floured surface; knead until smooth and elastic, about 4 minutes. Place in a well-greased bowl. Cover and let rise until doubled in bulk. Punch dough down, and divide into ten equal portions. Shape these portions into balls on a lightly floured surface and let rest 10 minutes. Roll out each ball to a 10-inch round. Place rounds on lightly greased baking sheets. Brush with cold water and sprinkle with sesame seeds. Do not allow to rise. Bake at 350 degrees for 25 minutes, or until lightly browned and crisp. Remove from pans and let cool on wire racks.

Yield: 10 cracker rounds.

Baklava

4 cups walnuts, coarsely ground

3 cups almonds, coarsely ground

1 cup sugar

2 tablespoons cinnamon

1 teaspoon allspice

½ teaspoon nutmeg

½ teaspoon ground cloves

2 cups (1 pound) butter

1 pound Phyllo (pastry sheets)

Whole cloves

Honey syrup (recipe on next page)

In a large bowl, mix nuts, sugar, cinnamon, allspice, nutmeg, and ground cloves. Brush bottom of a 12x18-inch baking pan with melted butter. Place six pastry sheets in bottom of pan, brushing each with butter. Sprinkle a thin layer of nut mix on top of the sixth buttered sheet. Cover with one sheet, brush with butter and sprinkle with nut mixture. Repeat, one for one, until all nuts are used. Top with six to eight sheets, placing one on top of the other (as in the beginning), and brushing each with butter. With a serrated knife, cut into strips 1-inch wide. Cut strips diagonally to form small diamond-shaped pieces. Place a whole clove in the center of each piece. Bake at 300 degrees for 2 hours (until lightly browned). Cover with honey syrup.

Honey Syrup

INGREDIENTS

3 cups sugar
3 cups water
1 tablespoon lemon juice
1½ cups honey
1 tablespoon vanilla

Boil sugar, water, and lemon juice for 15 minutes. Stir in honey and boil 15 minutes longer. Stir in vanilla. Set aside ¾ cup of syrup. Pour remaining boiling honey syrup slowly over hot baklava, right from the oven. Return baklava to 400 degree oven for 5 minutes exactly. Meanwhile boil ¾ cup reserved honey syrup for 5 minutes. Remove baklava from oven. Pour on syrup. Cool for 8 hours.

Yield: 9 dozen.

Neighborhood Winter Fest

Warm up even the coldest winter nights with laughter and friendship. The combined efforts of neighbors makes this party easy to plan and carry out. Even if it's warm where you live, this is an enjoyable activity. So, start a new tradition in your neighborhood.

IDEAS

• Using the idea of a progressive dinner, ask a few neighbors to help host a progressive outdoor winter party. Depending on the size of your neighborhood, everyone could either move from house to house as a group, or divide your guests into three groups and rotate. Let your guests know where to meet first. At each home, a fire in a portable fire pit or an old wheelbarrow welcomes and warms your guests.

• Just before the party begins line luminaries along the sidewalk of your neighborhood and also along the driveways of the people hosting the party.

A helpful idea is to give each neighbor the luminaries ahead of time and ask them to place and light the ones outside their home.

• For the activity at one of the homes, ask a friend that is an avid camera buff to come and take outdoor pictures of each couple or each family.

Extra lighting and a pine tree, snowman or interesting prop will help make the pictures perfect. As the guests are waiting for their turns, serve Snowball Soup (recipe follows). Complete with "homemade snowballs." After the party send each guest their picture in a festive paper frame found at stores that carry scrapbook supplies.

• At another house, serve piping hot Hearty Beef Stew and Cornbread.

• At still another house, provide the ingredients for S'mores and have the guests toast marshmallows over the coals in a fire pit.

• At the end of the party, the group could go caroling around other neighborhoods.

Menu

Hearty Beef Stew
Corn Bread
Snowball Soup
Homemade Snowballs
S´mores

Hearty Beef Stew

INGREDIENTS

4 pieces cubed beef steak

Flour to coat

2 tablespoons butter

½ cup chopped onion

2 packages (1.08 ounces each) brown gravy mix

4 cups water

2 packages frozen stew vegetables

½ cups frozen peas

Dredge steak in flour. Brown in butter in a large pot. Cut steak into small pieces and return to pot. Add onions and stir until onion is softened, not browned. Add water; sprinkle with gravy mix, and mix well. Cover; simmer for two hours. Add stew vegetables and continue simmering for one hour. Ten minutes before serving, add the peas to the stew.

Yield: 6 to 8 servings.

Corn Bread

INGREDIENTS
1 package yellow cake mix
1 cup yellow cornmeal
1 cup flour
3 tablespoons sugar
1 tablespoon baking powder
1 teaspoon salt
1/3 cup soft shortening, butter, or margarine
1 egg
1 cup milk

Preheat oven to 375 degrees. Prepare cake mix according to directions. Save half (2 cups) for cupcakes, etc. For corn bread, combine dry ingredients in bowl and mix well. Cut in shortening until well blended. Beat egg and milk together. Add to dry ingredients and blend slightly. Add cake batter to corn bread mixture. Blend thoroughly. Pour mixture into 2 greased square baking pans. Bake for 20 to 25 minutes.

Yield: 18 pieces.

Snowball Soup

I N G R E D I E N T S

10 cups instant powdered milk

1 jar (6 ounces) coffee creamer

1 can (16 ounces) instant chocolate drink mix

2 cups powdered sugar

Snowballs (marshmallows)

Chocolate chips

Mix together powdered milk, coffee creamer, chocolate drink mix, and powdered sugar. When ready for snowball soup, add 1/3 cup of mix in a cup of hot water. Top with snowballs (marshmallows) and sprinkle with chocolate chips. Keeps for as long as 6 months.

Yield: 15 cups mix or 45 cups Snowball Soup.

Homemade Snowballs

INGREDIENTS

Vegetable oil, for brushing

4 packages (3 tablespoons plus 1 teaspoon) unflavored gelatin

3 cups sugar

1¼ cups light corn syrup

¼ teaspoon salt

2 teaspoons vanilla extract

1½ cups powdered sugar

Brush a 9x13-inch glass baking dish with oil. Cut a piece of parchment or waxed paper large enough to cover the bottom of the dish and overhang the longer sides. Place in dish, brush with oil. Pour ¾ cup cold water in the bowl of an electric mixer, and sprinkle the gelatin on top. Let stand for 5 minutes. Place sugar, corn syrup, salt, and ¾ cup water in a medium saucepan. Set saucepan over high heat, and bring to a boil. Cook until mixture reaches softball stage (230 degrees), about 9 minutes. In a mixer, beat the hot syrup into gelatin at low speed. Gradually increasing speed to high, beat until mixture is very stiff (about 12 minutes). Beat in vanilla. Pour mixture into baking dish, and smooth the surface. Set aside, uncovered, until marshmallow becomes firm, at least 3 hours and up to overnight. Place 1 cup powdered sugar in a fine strainer, and sift onto a clean work surface. Invert large marshmallows onto sugar-coated surface, and peel off parchment paper. Lightly brush a sharp knife with vegetable oil, and cut marshmallows into twelve 2-inch squares. Sift the remaining ½ cup powdered sugar into a small bowl, and roll the marshmallows in the sugar to coat.

Yield: 12 snowballs.

A WORD About

Chocolate Lovers Only

Chocolate has long been associated with comfort and pleasure, but has suffered unjustly from the accusations of being the source of acne, tooth decay, weight gain, and heart disease. The findings are in, and chocolate has been cleared of many charges.

According to several recent studies, chocolate, in small amounts, can actually be beneficial. It contains antioxidants which thin the blood, protect the immune system, lower blood pressure, and may also prevent degenerative diseases such as cancer and heart disease. Dark chocolate is especially high in beneficial flavonoids.

Chocolate also contains a substance that is identical to a "happy hormone" manufactured by our bodies when we're in love. So chocolate can really "mend a broken heart" and elevate our spirits. It also contains large amounts of niacin, riboflavin, thiamine and B complex vitamins, and smaller amounts of vitamin A, phosphorate, potassium, calcium, protein, and iron.

There's even evidence an antibacterial substance in the cocoa bean actually helped prevent tooth decay.

It almost seems like chocolate is the latest health food, but don't overdo it. Only a small amount of chocolate, an ounce or two of a solid bar or a couple of tablespoons of cocoa—are needed to gain the positive effects. As it happens that is the exact amount needed for a soothing cup of hot chocolate. So curl up with a cup and enjoy!

CHOCOLATE FACTS

•Baking chocolate products will stay fresh for well over a year if stored in a cool, dry place (60 to 70 degrees).

• Cocoa keeps almost indefinitely when stored at room temperature in its original container. Avoid contact with moisture and high heat when storing. They can cause a gray discoloration or clumping, although neither affects the flavor or quality.

• Bloom, the gray film that sometimes appears on chocolate chips and bars, happens when chocolate is exposed to varying temperatures. It does not affect the taste or the quality of the chocolate.

• Cocoa may be used in place of unsweetened baking chocolate in most recipes. Three tablespoons of cocoa plus 1 tablespoon of shortening or oil equals 1 square (1 ounce) unsweetened chocolate.

• Do not substitute semi-sweet chocolate chips or milk chocolate chips for unsweetened baking chocolate.

• Measure cocoa by spooning it into a dry measuring cup; level with the edge of a knife or spatula.

• Chocolate scorches easily so melt chips or baking chocolate in a heavy saucepan, over a very low heat, stirring constantly; in the top of a double boiler, over hot water; or a minute at a time in the microwave oven.

• Condensation of steam droplets can cause chocolate to get stiff and grainy. If this occurs, stir in 1 teaspoon solid shortening (not butter) for every 2 ounces of chocolate.

Be A Whipping Cream Whiz

• Add powdered sugar to whipping cream before beating. The whipped cream stands up well, even if it is not used immediately.

• Whipping cream retains its shape longer if when whipping you add one teaspoon of light corn syrup for each half pint of cream.

• For whipping cream with a heavier texture that does not separate, add ¼ cup instant vanilla pudding mix along with powdered sugar and vanilla for each pint of cream.

• Try flavored whipping cream

Chocolate Whipped Cream

INGREDIENTS

1 pint heavy cream
3 heaping tablespoons cocoa mix
3 heaping tablespoons sugar
½ teaspoon vanilla extract

Combine all the ingredients in a bowl and whip with a mixer until the cream forms peaks.
Yield: 2 cups.

Nutmeg Whipped Cream

INGREDIENTS
½ cup whipping cream
1 tablespoon sugar
¼ teaspoon finely shredded orange peel
¼ teaspoon vanilla
⅛ teaspoon ground nutmeg

In a chilled small mixer bowl, combine all of the ingredients. Beat with chilled beaters of an electric mixer, on medium speed until soft peaks form. Serve immediately, or cover and chill till needed, up to 2 hours.

Yield: 1 cup.

Easy Lemon Cream

1 cup whipping cream
1 teaspoon vanilla
1 cup purchased lemon pudding

Beat whipping cream and vanilla until soft peaks form. Fold in lemon pudding and stir gently until combined. For a creamier texture stir in one tablespoon of lemon juice or milk.

Vanilla Bean Queen and Other Flavorings

Vanilla is one of the most familiar flavorings in our everyday foods. Vanilla comes from a rare species of the orchid family which produces a suitable bean only on a single day once a year. If the day is missed, a whole year must pass before another bean can be harvested. Once the bean is picked, it is immediately dipped into boiling water to stop its growth. Then it is placed in the sun to cure for six to nine months, inducing the subtle chemical changes that give vanilla its unique qualities.

Always use pure vanilla extract, rather than vanilla flavoring. The flavoring is made from vanillin, a crystalline phenolic aldehyde. Pure vanilla extract has a much stronger and pleasing flavor.

Store vanilla extract and vanilla beans in a cool dark place. Do not refrigerate them. Extract will keep several years, due to its alcohol content. Before storing, wrap beans in plastic and place inside an airtight container to keep in moisture.

To split a bean open, use a small, sharp paring knife and cut from one tip to the other. Carefully separate the two long, flat sides and scrape the seeds into the dish you're preparing. Save the pods for steeping or grinding to powder, or use them to make vanilla sugar.

When using other essences, always use the extract, not the flavoring. This rule of thumb also pertains to "real" chocolate chips rather than chocolate "flavored" chips.

About the Authors

Patricia F. Hemming is a consultant for national advertising firms. She and her daughter, Keely, have been working on this book since Keely was little—making lots of memories, sharing time cooking in the kitchen, and enjoying many family parties along the way. She is the coauthor of *Celebrate the Seasons*. She lives in Layton, Utah, with her husband, Michael, their daughter, Keely, and three miniature dachshunds.

Keely J. Hemming's love of cooking, reading, and family has naturally brought her to this point—writing a book with her mother. When she was little, she expressed the desire to be a "book lady." With the writing of this book and her job in a bookstore, she now is one. Keely has won several awards for her creative writing. She resides in Layton, Utah with her family.

The authors love to hear from their readers. You can e-mail them at phemming@thebluezone.net or khemming@thebluezone.net.

0 26575 78871 6